# WORLD OF JOY



Compiled by
Chandrika J.N and Gopal Krishna Deb

Published By
Creativity United

# TITLE : WORLD OF JOY

**Author's name : Chandrika J.N And Gopal Krishna Deb**

**Published by : Creativity United**

HN : 52, Main road, Kayasthagram,
Karimganj – 788719

Email: unitedwecreateabetterworld@gmail.com

ISBN: 978-81-952726-5-5

POETRY 1st Edition

# PREFACE

The presented book "World Of Joy" is a shared literary collection. We the compilers Chandrika J.N and Gopal Krishna Deb greet all the readers with all warmth. "World Of Joy" has a special purpose in its name. It is said that, "the world is full of pain", but everyone has their own perspective to see this world and here we have tried to show the positive side of that perspective. In this literary collection, the authors, who have written on this very topic, had tried to show their perspective of their world with the connection of joy through their mentioned writeups; in form of short-story, poetry, mini personal blurbs etc. This collection contains the writings of a few selected authors.

Hope "World Of Joy" will be enjoyable and resourceful for the readers.

Thank you

*Gopal Krishna Deb*

*Chandrika J.N*

( Compilers )

# INDEX

# COMPILER'S INTRODUCTION

## CHANDRIKA J.N

"Laughing is heaven" , by this words I would like to introduce MS. Chandrika.J.N, Author of this anthology . She was born and raised in karnataka . Writing has been her passion and published her content in many anthologies. A sixteen year old girl who is inspired by fresh thoughts her love towards literature turned her into a writer. Writing has been her new found companion in this mysterious world. She loves penning her thoughts in a piece of paper. You can contact her through, Email address: Chandrikajn866@gmail.com

# GOPAL KRISHNA DEB

"Life is a process of continuous learning, and I am just a learner."
____G.K.D.

The author Gopal Krishna Deb is a college lecturer by profession. He is a resident of Kayasthagram in Karimganj district of India. He is interested in composing, analyzing and exploring different dimensions of linguistics. He likes to learn and write in different forms of literature.

**Take a deep breath reader…**

**It's going to be an amazing time from now on……**

# AASTHA PRASAD

## 1. "A world of strange people"

A world of stangers
A world of new people
A world of new fear
Fear at glance
Everybody seems a bad pupil!
Bad intentions trapped in,
Our faces grow gloomy seeing outsiders.
Heart beats loud.
Seem like a world of complete loss!

A world in which hopes volatile
A world who is not like me
A world which is new
Will they accept me?
Will they not do something wrong with me?
Will they keep away their hands for rape don't comes into play?
Will there be anyone to hear my cry?
Will they treat me inferior then them?
As am a new here?
There are no limit to questioning.

A world which is strange
A world which is foreign for me
A world which is different
Have we questioned ourself ever
The same horror is faced by the opposite side.

World Of Joy

Our beloved friends today,
Were the  strangers one day.
But they care about us!
And **frame a world of joy!**
So foreign land of strange people will be there.
Judge them the same way_
For they are no one different from us.
Mom's advice don't talk to strangers_
Are we following it -no,
If yes, than we would have no friends!
Even our mom's tend to unfollow it,
For she too have friends!!

© Aastha Prasad.

# ABHISHEK KUSHWAH

## 1. "My Dear Solace"

In the world of Joy
there is too much space
But I need nothing instead of your solace.

In my heart your place can't be replace.
You are one who give me solace in my life.
You are definitely ace friend in my life.

Every pain will be erase when you're my solace.
Your embrace is such a grace my dear solace.
Love you a lot My Dear solace........
Love you a lot My Dear solace...........

## 2. "Introspection"

It is very horror ...........
when I look myself in mirror
because a lot of error in myself appear.
It's a big dare to compare myself to myself.

To build up your potential
introspection is very essential.
Because it is a switch to on
the power of own.
The best direction to move on is introspection.
It is the best direction to achive perfection in this world of Joy.

© Abhishekh Kushwah.

## 3. "The evening is too Melancholic"

The truth is too Vitriolic,
Every night becomes too alcoholic.
If the evening is melancholic.
Stay happy is just symbolic.
Because the relationship is abolish.
This evening is too melancholic.

It depend on how you pretend
When I silently cry inside.
I'm not happy but satisfied.
To express pain everytime is not justified.
However I don't feel comfortable in world of joy without you,
However My pain is Uncountable.

This evening is too melancholic
The shine is no more that you polish.
That's why the evening is melancholic.

© Abhishekh Kushwah.

# ABHIPSA BHOI

## 1. "SWEETHEART"

You are my Love
And love is blind...
In this world of Joy...
I know my Babe,
You are so kind.
Guide me beauty,
You're my cuty.
Let me enter to your heart,
My sweetheart.
Look at my eyes,
There're only Love.
Don't force to quit me,
Dear, It's my job.
Guide me beauty,
You're my cuty.
Let me enter to your heart,
My sweetheart.
My sweetheart.

## ADEKOYA AYOOLA

### 1. "My world of Joy"

I come into this world in tears
If I don't cry they force me to; it's a necessity
People on whites pry into my privacy
Newborn me can't even get some privacy; To see the world I have newly stepped into
Or should I say, pulled into

I grow up and my life begins to gain some joy after all
But all that play and fantasy don't last
You gotta work
People see a happy man and they say," His works are dirty", "He's into blood money"

When you cry,
People say,"She's got no love"
Our own Soil can't even grant us some joy
In this world, you ain't free to do what you wish
You laugh,it's a problem
You cry, it's a predicament

I don't want to end my life in the way I came in; in tears
I want to jubilate in steady joy while my heart beats it's last
The World of Joy is what I seek

© Adekoya ayoola.

## 2. "My World of Joy"

I come into this world in tears
If I don't cry they force me to; it's a necessity
People on whites pry into my privacy
Newborn me can't even get some privacy; To see the world I have newly stepped into
Or should I say, pulled into

I grow up and my life begins to gain some joy after all
But all that play and fantasy don't last
You gotta work
People see a happy man and they say," His works are dirty", "He's into blood money"

When you cry,
People say,"She's got no love"
Our own Soil can't even grant us some joy
In this world, you ain't free to do what you wish
You laugh,it's a problem
You cry, it's a predicament

I don't want to end my life in the way I came in; in tears
I want to jubilate in steady joy while my heart beats it's last
The World of Joy is what I seek

© Adekoya ayoola.

## 3. "My World of Joy"

I come into this world in tears
If I don't cry they force me to; it's a necessity
People on whites pry into my privacy
Newborn me can't even get some privacy; To see the world I have newly stepped into
Or should I say, pulled into

I grow up and my life begins to gain some joy after all
But all that play and fantasy don't last
You gotta work
People see a happy man and they say," His works are dirty", "He's into blood money"

When you cry,
People say,"She's got no love"
Our own Soil can't even grant us some joy
In this world, you ain't free to do what you wish
You laugh,it's a problem
You cry, it's a predicament

I don't want to end my life in the way I came in; in tears
I want to jubilate in steady joy while my heart beats it's last
The World of Joy is what I seek

© Adekoya ayoola.

# ALKAMA

## 1. "World of joy"

If this great world of joy and pain
Revolve in one sure track;
If freedom, set, will rise again,
And virtue, flown, come back;
Woe to the purblind crew who fill
The heart with each day's care;
Nor gain, from past or future, skill
To bear, and to forbear!

© Alkama.

# AMARJEET SINGH

## 1. "Try Try Again in this world of joy"

If at first step you don't succeed
Then don't supersede
Try Try Again
If you find your goal is far
Just do wirk hard and you will be superstar
Try Try Again
To do anything,firstly your courage should appear
Drive away your fear
Try Try Again
If you get some pain
It means you are able to gain
Try Try Again.

## AMIRTHAVARSHINI.K.J

### 1.

In this world of joy!
I will be by your side,
You are more than what I deserve...
I met you as an accident
Have you as the best forever...
I insult you
I slap you
I fight with you
And also I fight for you ✨
Moment you spent with others makes me feel possessive

When you are with me its marked as a memory...
I promise you that
Not gonna allow anyone to hurt you
If happens...
I will not allow you to face it alone

In This world of joy
We face a great medical war
Mask in your emotions...
Walk in your homes
Start Sanitized
Keep donating
Stay vaccinated...

Hope for the day
We hug each other...

## World Of Joy

Walkout without masks
The world is back to normal
Humans of the world with humanity again...

In this world of joy
Lots of people around,
I think of you
Day and night
Smile like an idiot
With your memories...

You are not my love
Not my friend
Not my dad
Not my blooded brother

But you stand for me
Hold my hands when I lay back...
Pull me up when I fall...
My sedative
My stress burster
My life line.

# AYUSH MONDAL

## 1. "EDUCATION"

If you consider properly that
Education is a basic need
Then you should consider that
Everybody has the proper right
His education is equal to her education
It's your narrow thought that
What she can do in future?
She will be educated for her needs
It has no eyes to make boundaries
It never judges anybody
It provides itself to everybody
It can't see who's boy or girl
It can't tell who's young or old
It can't hear who's poor or rich
Everybody need it as a human right in this world of joy...
If it's not possible to take it
Then be ready for the brain fight
You can buy anything from money
But, Education is so precious that
Only they can achieve who can get.

## 2. "Take a relief in world of joy"

It's time to take relief
I said always try to feel
but you wouldn't believe
There's no relief even in air,
People are fighting and
Facing the today's situation
They're so brave and dare,
You can try to take yourself
Then, take yourself so much care
We think only few can survive
But it's reality in case of rare,
So don't give anyone to use
Your handkerchief, don't try to share
Always try to cover your mouth
With your mask, don't keep it bare
All doctors are providing informations
Please, listen properly with your ear
All pains are inside in the heart
Don't fill it with future fear,
Announcement are made in local areas
But it seems, you don't want to hear
It will enter in you, through
The people who is sitting in near,
So don't go anywhere outside
Just take relief in house inside.

# AMAN RAJ

## 1. "My Guiding light"

Let's talk about the one, who we actually take for granted !

My Guiding light in this "world of joy",
She who gave me comfort, had gone through many sacrifices built a bed of roses while thorns pricked her beautiful hands she barely ate something to fill my empty stomach saved every drop of water, to quench my thirst left her favourite dish, to fulfill my cravings made me delicacies, before I even expressed always knew what I felt, when the entire world left me alone never minded my rude behaviour, and just walked away with a smile always when I shouted at her and my anger burst out she never left my hand she who has her own life, forgot completely about it she who has her dreams, never even thought about it she who wanted to be something, is now preparing me for the same beyond imagination is her love always smiled in front of me while she was weeping near the stove she protected me from the scavenger in the universe and taught me what it takes to fight never laughed at my fear, but told that I am always with you dear I fell down may be a thousand times, and she picked me up and told your scars are all mine I know that if this were a loan, I would definitely default because the abundant love you shower on me is more than the infinity you never demanded anything for yourself selflessly, just said aim to be a remarkable person whatever I am today, is all because of you if you weren't here mummy, what would I even do without you?

## 2. "The Conventional form of wealth"

"One human life is worth more than all treasures of earth"- the saying definitely holds to be really true. The year 2020 made us to understand how it is health and not wealth which is a necessity. Ever since the outbreak of the pandemic this year every now and then circumstances have made us realise that be it for having strong immunity, or by distancing ourselves from the masses, or by hitting the lowest in career prospect. Compromising with health can increase your chances to deal with bigger consequences in the near future. Including physical activities like exercise, walking, cycling can be of a fun and beneficial as well. It is us who can also take initiative to start with gardening. To have a small kitchen garden, which will help us to get a few organic vegetables and also seeing the green plants will eventually help us to uplift the mood.

Can we not take this opportunity to provide ourselves with the happiness of plucking our own vegetables or fruits, or to give our eye the privilege of gazing at some beautiful flowers.....!!

A small step towards change the "world of joy" and better health begins from us. This year 2020 is to make ourselves realise the importance of nature and to get involved in creating it. Finally to conclude, starting a age long proverb known to all..." HEALTH IS WEALTH"

© Aman Raj.

## 3. "Patriotism"

We all are indians first....
History is our witness,
And martyrs are the god,
We are disciples of gurus,
This land is saints' abode.
Compassion is our heritage;
In humanity do we trust,
Neither hindu nor Muslim,
We all are indians first.
Diversity is our culture,
And unity is our strength,
We strive for peace of world, but are cautious of defence.
Challenger of our sovereignty in the world of joy ,
For sure would bite the dust,
Neither Kann

© Aman Raj.

# ANGELA MERLIN C

## 1. "Seventh Heaven"

How would it be to live in a world ?
Where there are no discriminations,
Where everyone are treated alike,
and where people live in Peace and Harmony.

Where there are no set rules,
Where women are never subjugated
In the name of custom and traditions
and where she is treated equal to Men.

Where there are no Murder cases,
Where People doesn't know the meaning of the Word "Stress",
Where intoxicating isn't the only pain killer,
and where People live their life as they wish.

Where there are no Bio-Wars,
but only Love-Wars,
Where there are no weapons and Swords,
and where only Love is the powerful weapon.

Where there are no Rape Victims,
Where people never knew the meaning of the word "Rape"
Where there are no Green-eyed monsters - Jealousy
and where people live their life to the fullest.

Where falling in Love with a person of other caste

World Of Joy

Isn't a big crime,
and where transgender's are allowed to get Married
to the person whom they like.

Where Marriages are literally a fairy tale,
Where people don't demand any dowries,
Where daughters-in-law are treated as daughters,
and sons-in-Law are treated as Sons.

Where there are no Old age homes,
Instead the elders are taken care by their own children,
Where there are no Orphanges for Girl children,
and where Parents raise their child without any differentiation.

It sounds really Great to live in such a beautiful world right?
The so called WORLD OF JOY,
The so called SEVENTH HEAVEN,
Where only Ecstasy prevails.

It is only in our hands to create such a joyful World,
Let the change begin with us,
Eventually the others will change,
and together Let's create a "WORLD OF JOY".

© Angela Merlin C

## 2. "The Real Ecstasy"

If, Smoking can give happiness,
Intoxication can give happiness,
Injecting drugs can give happiness,
What happiness do we give to our parents?

It took nine whole months for our Mom to introduce us to the whole world
It took 17 whole years for our Dad to let us stand on our own.
It took our parents their entire life time to care for us and love us unconditionally,
Will all these drugs and alcohol make them happy?

Literally it hurts them the most.
Introduce them to the World of Joy
Where you can give the purest form of happiness and Love,
Which they will cherish forever.

© Angela Merlin C

# G. ANITEE DELAITTA

## 1. "Stages of joy"

Depressed in life, losing faith and hope, crying in one corner of the room, rishu was thinking about the decisions she made in her life. Having decided that there is no more joy or happiness in her life, she gave up on everything. She got up hearing her phone ringing, before she could attend it , the call gets ended. She sighed and looked down. There was a surprise to her in big box , it was very dusty. It wasn't opened from years. She sat down and tried to open the box very quickly and finally it brought a smile on her face admist all her worries. First she saw her first standard note book, she thought of the joy when she got full marks in her dictation. Then she smiled seeing her handwriting when she was young. Next she saw photographs of her and her friends. Thinking how small she was that time and how much fun she had experiencing small new things, it made her feel good and gave her hope. Then she saw all the certificates she got for singing. She thought to herself how hard she worked from scratch. Singing has been her joy in this whole world but now she decided to give up because of her circumstances. Seeing the certificates gave her a different feeling of happiness and sadness. As she was seeing them she found a note which was written by her when she was young. The note said, " Rishu the great singer, don't give up until you achieve". It felt like as thought she wrote it for her new self. Thinking how much singing had given her joy, she decided to start again . Again she heard her phone ringing and this time she attended it. The person in the phone said that she is selected for the main vocal in a big movie. Speechless and not knowing what to do she just said thank you and kept her phone. She was very happy that she found her world of joy and promised that she will not give up again. She also realised that she experienced joy in all stages of life even though there where a lot of obstacles and circumstances.

## 2. "Joyful world"

Sometimes we try to find joy in the world,
Forgetting that the world itself is a joy.
Sometimes we try to find joy in someone else, forgetting that
your mere existence is a joy to someone.
Again , The world itself is a joy and the world of joy is you.

© G. Anitee Delaitta.

## 3. "Joy"

The little one asked, " What is joy".
Her mom answered, " You are ".
My little world of joy

© G. Anitee Delaitta.

# ARUNIMA BAHADUR KHARE

## 1. "Search of joy"

I was in search of joy,
I found all materialistic thing as a toy,
They gave me no joy,
I found there,no enjoy.
I was upset,
It was my test,
To search world of joy,
I need no toy.
I searched old tradition,
Found depth in meditation,
It was an inward journey,
Made life full of hormony
It was the world of joy,
Which I searched in lots of toys.
I found happiness within me,
Inner world is full of glory.
Now search was complete,
I found everything I need,
Now,I am always happy,
Want to make everyone happy.

## 2. "Good deed"

Everyone was busy,
To make life easy,
No love,no relation,
No place for emotion.
Life was so dry,
Made them to cry,
Luxury but no joy,
They made themselves a toy,
Running and running,
only for earning
They found nothing,
Lost everything,
I was also among them,
Made my own name.
Once I saw a crying baby,
Her dress was shabby,
She was an orphan,
Destiny made her alone.
I went to her,
To earn happiness for her,
I adopt her as my child,
It looks world so wide,
Now,my world was full of joy,
Good deed made the life to enjoy,
It was world of joy,
Which I enjoy.

## 3. "True happiness"

I was in depth of selfishness,
Life was full of dryness,
Materialistic thing made me mad,
I was sad,
Everything was here,
But no joy forever,
No feelings,no relation,
I lost all emotions.
I met a poor family,
Struggle was their destiny,
But their faces was bright,
A pause was at this sight,
I went there,
To see all affair,
They lived with emotion,
Life was in relation.
There world was full of joy,
Although they have no materialistic toy.
I stopped there and learn more
Relations grows happiness more.
It is the basis of world of joy,
Each and everyone can enjoy.

# ASMA RAJ

## 1. "Joy : A way to Happy Life"

The world of joy for you should be,
Where you find peace and happiness...

Find joy in each and everything you do,
Otherwise everything is useless what you did...

Always be joyous from your heart,
Like this you can heal each and every person...

Sometimes your joy is the reason of your smile,
And when you smile your whole world blooms with happiness...

Joy is something which comes from within,
When you do the work of your choice, it makes you feel good...

Let your joy be in experiencing the journey,
Not in finishing and completing it on time...

# ARSHAD RAJ

## 1. "The World of Joy"

How beautiful is the nature?
God has created all the creatures.

The nature in the rainy season.
Look beautiful to all the persons.

The plants enjoying in the rain.
The peacock dancing in the rain.

The rivers flowing full of strength.
And Cuckoo singing in the rain.

The sound of the falling rain.
Gives inner peace to my brain.

I Feel The world of joy.
Of nature in the rain.

## ASHITA SHARMA

### 1. "An Open Sky"

Its a beautiful world of joy,
beneath is the power of land while,
above resides a vast open sky.

Its a happy colourful place,
without any man's greed or human race.

It has fulltime dreamers,
It has strong believers.
There are dreamy eyes and,
birds with open wings,
flying high in blue skies.

It has tall and strong trees ,
green leaves dancing to and fro,
with the movement of breeze.

The land beneath tells a truthful tale,
but the clouds have a mystery no can tell.

Bucket full of dreams, which the eyes treasure,
the white sky keeps those dreams safe forever.

Truely, its a beautiful world of joy,
beneath is the power of land while,
above resides a vast open sky.

## 2. "The beauty of words"

These days I have realised that there is nothing more beautiful than "words ".

The words have a great impact in my life these days,some phrases,some poems,some quotes seems so relatable.

Just a few words and my life gets summarised with them, just few words which make me happy , which make me cry.

People say words have a power to break you or make you but then a few words will make you see a "New you ".

Truely, the world of words is a beautiful place to be in, its my world of joy, my paradise.

© Ashita Sharma.

## 3. "Embracing the darker shade in world of joy"

Darkness is tough to deal with but when the light fails to enlighten our life,
when there is nothing in this world that seems alright, in these times,

the colours fade, the shades fade,
and such times teaches us,
to embrace those darker shades.

Being in the dark world of gloominess,
we may feel scared at times, in begininng
but slowly we learn to live in this world,
eventually, we learn to love the dark in pieces.

It may not be a complete world of joy for all,
but oneday, everyone has to stay strong & tall.

Its tough to Embrace the darker shade when light doesnt pass the narrow hole of life.

But when the colours fade to touch the soul,
these darker shades help in dealing with life.

# AVINASH CHANDRA JHA

## 1. "My Munchkin"

It feels truly blessed when
your tiny little head placed carelessly
on my left shoulders,
Your right palm holding me from around
Whereas left one on my chest
While lying down after a hectic day at work
It feels like being nurtured and pampered
With every touch of yours, my munchkin.
From being notorious to cry baby, the whole day
You ultimately find solace on my body
Gifting the world of joy to me.

## 2. "Moment Of Joy"

Resting on my arm chair
a novel kept on my belly
and eyes shut
I felt this sudden connection to her
whom I just met a page back
And then all of a sudden
She took the pair of glasses off me
Placing them exact near my night lamp
Her fingertips passing the eyes and lips
were along my throat
And then I lost it
Lost all senses of restraints and judgement
I just went into this extraordinary experience
where I felt Nothing but love
Just pouring into my body
down to my thighs, legs and feet
gradually feeling wet on my feet
I got uncomfortable and sulkier now
My eyes opened to a surprise
The little puppy licking it with love
I smiled picking him to my lap
Kissing and pampering him all around
For a moment led me to my world of joy.

© Avinash Chandra Jha.

## 3. "Past Instances"

Heart broken and shattered now
Weeping all the time
I just recall all the past instances
When I would feel happy and delighted
Even after facing hardships throughout the day
Your one smiling face was healer
while welcoming me at the door
And potentially create a world of joy within me.

# BANDITA SAHU

## 1. "The World I Seek"

The world of joy,
Which money can't ever buy..
It's the spirit that comes from depth of heart,
It's the reason why Earth has never fallen apart..

© Bandita Sahu.

## 2. "The World Of Joy"

One day I saw a little boy,
His smile carried the whole world's joy..
And then I realized, there's no specific reason to be happy,
As long as you're happy just as a baby..

© Bandita Sahu.

## 3. "Joyous World"

One day I saw,
Withering in cold, one little paw..
I was just going near him, when an poor old man took and made him sleep with him,
I realized "the world of joy"s true meaning..

© Bandita Sahu.

# BHARGAVI. V

## 1. "Worth remembering world of joy"

Some days in our life
Are really worth remembering..
Some seconds are meant to hurt
Some hearts are meant alone to cry
Even some words are meant to hurt
But only the true loyal souls
Are meant for worthy remembering ever..
Tidying up the tongue doesn't mean
Those words are gold..
Moulding up the silver never
Worth as a platinum..
So create the days in your life
That are worth to remember..

©Bhargavi. V

## 2. "New beginnings"

There is always a path
In this world
In this beautiful world of joy
Helping people to feel the warmth
Like a diamond so old..

Filled with treasures
This life needs more glories
Triggered with ruthless pressures
This stage brings more worries..

Flattering oneself is not a big deal
Featuring the inner self creates
A bigger shield..
Flawless lives are like crater free moon.
Only the moon will be seen beautiful
With those little craters
From this far land...

©Bhargavi. V

## 3. " Not in my hand "

The real mirth of life
Lies in failures...
The joyous part begins
When one fails..
This is not false
This is the truth...
One cannot taste
The presidential essence of success
Until having bitten by the venomous poison...
Live or die
But before that know
Their meaning and find
A best way to select and start..
To understand this world of joy..

©Bhargavi. V

## BHRIGU SONI

### 1. "World of joy"

HEY...Love can't be expressed in one paragraph or in some words if we start expressing our feeling it would be endless... Well, LOVE is a feeling a magic it can have different meaning for different people. Love is the key to happiness we all want to lead a happy life. People look around for happiness in power,fashion,wealth etc...But these things can only give you temporary pleasures Em i right?? The power of love can create Miracles. Love can create unity among nations and its citizens. Love is the most beautiful feeling in the world. Love has given different meaning by different people depending upon how they have experienced this wonderful feelings. You are always available for the person whom you love. Love knows no boundaries. Love makes you to do the best things for your loved ones to make them feel happy & proud about themselves. When you love someone you accept their weekness too and love them for whatever they are. Love has no specific meaning. Love is the most important aspect of an individuals life. Love also carries harsh feelings sometimes but still it is considered as one of the best feeling in the world. love isn't just a feeling.. it's something you know. its that feeling when you first wake up and you think instinctively of that one person, it's the urge to want to be with someone, it's the person you go to with all your problems.. the only person you want to talk to after a long day, it's the one thing you know is always true.. yes sometimes it leads to heartbreak, but it may not. don't fear love.. Trust the people who love you. Be happy with them. Give something to them in return. Make them feel happy too. Love them back. Protect them too if required.....!!

## 2. "Hope"

Hope helps us to ignore the sufferings of the present in the "world of joy". When we stay positive about our future, and feel that we have to fight to win the problems, our probability to succeed increases. It happens because we fight trying to stay mentally strong and give our best efforts. Hope is a belief. You believe something good will happen. The intensity of this feeling can really change your present and future. It's said hope, which is also your belief, is a deep sense hidden in our subconscious mind.

Remember that our subconscious mind is the most powerful thing on this earth. With its help, you can make an impossible possible, or win a war, for example.A true hope or belief is unbreakable. There are many theories regarding the pure definition of hope. But you don't have to confuse yourself with so many opinions. Just ask yourself – what you belief. If you believe to have something good in the future, and expect it to happen, that is hope. When you keep yourself telling that there will be no more pain.

# CHETAN SUTAR

## 1. "Some thing we need"

Hope there's some time
As I never got a fraction of it
A pickle of sweet lime
As a present to the neighbour

Heads down to the attractive brightness
Forgot the space shown above
In the corner, leave alone the stres
To experience the latest events

Think about thoughts of tomorrow
It's wrong to die today
In the corner, leave alone the sorrow
To breathe in the world of joy
Taking leave
To the ride of heaven

## 2. "Jump start for height"

Never thought would lose myself ...
Keep working on it without any reason ...
I left my dream which made me cry...
In the world of joy, I had faced tears...
Look up high, face the danger...!
Don't push me back, let me try...

© Chetan Sutar.

## 3. "Garden on fire"

It was last night...
I never imagined the sight ...
My world of joy...
Was set on fire...

Look at the vigorous flares ...
Became the destructive snares...
My lovely Garden...
Was set on fire...

© Chetan Sutar.

## DIKSHA AGARWAL

### 1. "World Of Joy"

The world of joy
has vast meaning.
It differs from man to man.
For me,
world of joy is my parents,
if my parents are happy,
then I am happy.

When a child is born,
it's a matter of joy for the parents.

When an unemployed,
gets a job?
it's a matter of joy for him.
When a sports person wins a medal,
it's a matter of joy for them!
When a child gets success in the exam,
it's a matter of joy for the parents always.

For me,
my world of joy
is being happy with my parents...

# DIPTI DAVID

## 1. "World of Joy"

A world like no other,
a world where you need no money.
A world where you don't need anything,
a world where you don't need anyone.
A world where you need not shed a tear,
in a world where you need not feel depressed.
In a world where you need not feel stressed.
A world where you can be totally free.
Is a "world of joy."

## 2. "A world of Melancholic Glee"

A world that is a mixture of good and bad
where everything is bitter-sweet.
Where everything is smooth
And rough at the same time.
A world that is a combination;
of two sides or many shades.
A world of melancholy and glee,
is a world that is not only a "world of Joy,"
but a world of sorrow and joy.

© Dipti David.

## 3. “A world of wonder and wander”

A world where you can wander,
wondering about this world of wonder.
The world of wonder in which you can roam around for a while.
A world of joy that lasts for a while,
the world of wonder and wanders.

© Dipti David.

## Divyadharshini. R

### 1. "Adventure travel"

Everyone has a problem in this world.
Every day we face obstacles so rude.
Every hour human's mood will be changing as a see-saw...
Every minute, life shows a different way to what we saw...
"All the world's a stage...
And all the men and women merely players"
These words are spoken by Shakespeare...
Yeah.! The true system is to appear...
Happy or sad...
Just go with a hopeful hand...
There are much variety of persons...
From them, we learn many lessons...
The combination of thunder and lightning
Beautiful drops come to earth...
The combination of pleasure and suffering
The world of joy comes to breath
Merry and melancholy don't get to suffer...
Just go like a river...
The world of joy is a driver
Making us an adventurous rover...

## 2. "Just explore"

One says life is full of pains and problems...
One says life is full of surprise and miracles
But I say life is the world of joy...
One day sincerely one day...
Put away your worries
Just explore the world.
With no care frees...
That one day, it's not long...
Today or tomorrow...
One day will come to explore...
Our fantastic joyful journey
I'm ready to start...
Are you ready to venture
The world with delight...?

© Divyadharshini. R.

## 3. "Companion"

When I see your eyes
I start to say lies
When I pick your lips
It a crunchy chips
You are the queen of my kingdom
I'm the king of your bosom
Come with me as a companion
To reveal the joy with a union...
You are my better half...
Are you ready to accept me as another half
Love our life with joy...
Live our life in the world of joy

© Divyadharshini. R.

# DIVYANSHI

## 1. "Remember"

At twenty one thirty ,
and far away,
she made up her mind
and couldn't stay.

Her pain was too much,
for her to bear
I tried to reach out,
but she didn't care.

At just seventeen,
she had been through hell,
Could not escape
her molested cell.

Nowhere to go,
seeing darkness around,
No escape for this girl,
only hell bound.

I begged her to stay,
she said go away,
Why do you care?
I bowed down to pray.

She grabbed the blade,

going deeper every time,
Slashed her wrist,
I cried and I cried.

A thousand miles away,
I am now in somber.
Why did you leave me?
I will always remember.

©Divyanshi patha.

## 2. "Flashback"

Memories are dead rose. You turn them over and over, until one day to come over a piece of broken frame and when you look through the tears in your eye.

You realise there were more cracks in your relationship but you were happy when you were with her.

Like a rose kept inside torn pages of those leather bound handwritten copy of Pablo.

©Divyanshi patha.

## 3. "I wanna die"

"I wanna die
But it is not that death in which the heart stops
And the body becomes cold
And equal to the Earth
I wanna die
But not to not hear a sound
No sun rises above me
I cannot look
To the moon and the stars
I want to die an extraordinary death
Dying like turning water into steam
And like sowing seeds
Like sunrise
Like turning the sky into clouds
I want to annihilate
To appear in another world
A world not yet taken
A world I have never tried before
Like a fantasy world
It has everything normal
Only the fear of annihilation
And fear of impotence
Fear of loneliness ".

©Divyanshi patha.

## EKTA GUPTA

# 1. "The World of joy"

"They say a person needs just three things to be truly happy in this world: someone to love, something to do, and something to hope for."
— Tom Bodett

Life is so beautiful, nature is so beautiful , every animal or bird is so beautiful and what here I want to convey here is that god creations are all beautiful and it's our vision and upto us they how do we look at a particular life, nature or animal.

Isn't it we always try to blame our own sorrows and sad feeling to others that because of this person this happened in my life, but in reality and deeper thought if one can analyze when our own mind is at peace after a big fight then our soul speaks silently and there is one voice start speaking to ourselves (One would have noticed in movies – a image is shown in mirror –like our inner self starts talking to oneself – I hope u all can relate to it perfectly and a smile appears on your face saying "ya" aisa hota hai humare saath ) So now we could understand that it`s our own mind and way of reacting to other`s behavior ad what matter most important is how we try to respond to a situation we are in.

So instead of us blaming others and our situation, one needs to analyses what is our word of joy. However the fast digital world and fast pacing life has changed so much. Earlier when there were no smart phones .One human use to value other human much but nowadays people got a tendency to search on google o se you tube channel for any advice. So the love and affection

which use to exists between family members, friends and groups have al got lost somewhere.
We humans now tend to forget that our happiness use to lies in small and minute things and not in big materialistic thing or no on how many likes did we get on facebook post or instapost
If you are being love by someone then remember you are the luckiest person in this world
Spend time with family talking to them one`s heart out and set your goal in life and set a target to you goal and hope for that your goal will be achieved sooner or later.

© Ekta Gupta.

## 2. "Circle of life"

Be always joyous,
No matter what
Life is precious
Not the anger or any situation,
Trust god rather than the person,
And your journey will be marvelous
Do remember nothing lasts long
Neither the good nor the worst`s
U will realize that is a circle
And not the end of "the world of joy"

# GARGI GHOSH

## 1. "She is everything"

She is everything
Yes,she is everything in the "world of joy".
She is my darling mother
She is my best friend

Without her I am nothing
Without her I'm totally blind
Want to quarrel with her
Want to love my darling

My Darling “MOM”
My first love
My unconditional love

Who protects me from
Any kind of storm,
Any kind disturbance,
She can't leave me.
She is my faith
Whom I love blindly.

Definitely "SHE IS EVERYTHING"

## 2. "Pain to Gain in world of joy "

Some flower must grow through dirt......
The more you are hurt,
The more you will change.
It makes you,
Strong stronger strongest.
When we are hurt,
We learn.
So,stay focus your purpose,
Not your pain.
Change comes with pain.
It explains very well.
No pain no gain.
Frustration is quite painful,
But it's a very essential part of our success.
Pain is a great motivator.
No gain without pain.
We know all about this.
Everybody wants happiness.
Nobody wants pain.
We can't have a rainbow,
Without a little rain.

© GARGI GHOSH

## 3. "You & me in world of joy "

Hey..!! my Love....
I want to go with you.
Where just you & I
You & me always.

Take my hand
Take my whole life too.
You are the finest,
Loveliest, tenderest,
Most beautiful person,
In the World.

It's always better
When we're together.
You are my world.
My soul & your soul
Forever Tangled.

Our Love is like a wind.
Can't see it.
But I can feel it.

© Gargi Ghosh

## GEETHIKA REDDY

### 1. "Doctors - the reason for celebration of being alive !!!"

Doctors are the world of joy,
Injecting positive vibes in us today to enjoy,
Their thoughts
hearing our heart beat with their creative instrument,
With the wisdom of subject they cures all the ailments,
Physician nature is filled with heart of patience,
His bewildering profession make us to bleed quotations,
A surgeon hands is filled with magic of motivation,
Tho' if we pay tons of love we can't beat the debt of his dedication,
A medic gets fully stressed day in and day out,
They always provide helping hands to save humanity without doubt,
A doc will have aorta(largest part in heart) of colourful garden,
Pouring healthy life into new offspring is their happiness of carton,
Doctor's bleed day and night telling it's our sanity and honour,

In return their sacrifice of adventure make this
world stronger,
Saluting all the physcians whole heartedly today on
this special day,
Hope you all will rest in peace and reborn again to
create a way,
Dear medicos you are and were the real warriors of
this life game,
Today I'm taking dignity to ink this poem on your
archive with inflame.

© Geethika Reddy

# IPSA SWAIN

## 1. "Some Memories are Shattered"

What if one day our memories get all shattered. All these valuable things will get vanished from this Mortal world. Rich and poor both will look same, and our Ego will eventually find its own dustbin. Class struggle will become Pluto which will vanish forever from its orbit. Then there will be no Tradition or Culture or no boundaries will bind us. No geographical limitations can limit us. The day will come everyone feels the same. It will be difficult to find who are my parents and who are yours. Because, everyone resembles each other and all their actions are same.

No one's going to remember, not the Plato, Aristotle or any Vishnu or Shiva. Because everyone is going to drink the water of river Lethe. There will be no future and there will be no past. The time that is with us not even our present. There will be no vicissitudes in life. There will be no one to believe in God and no one is going to remember the cruel Devil. Even the Eden garden is going to turn into an Exile garden. No Forbidden fruit will be there. Neither Brahma nor Vishnu is going to grow a lotus flower from Vishnu's navel with Brahma sitting on it. Every Religious place will turn into a barren woman. There is no footfall anywhere.

There will be no one to perform in the stage of Shakespeare. World will be full of Fossils, not of Dinosaur, but of Humans. No one is going to be the last person of the world or no one is going to deliver their last message to the world. Science will become handicapped, neither physics nor any law will be there. All memories will get shattered. Everyone will forget Einstein and Homer neither any formula will bring back nor any scripture can bring back memory.

Everyone is lying side-to-side. But, no one has the courage to face anyone. Life is just about few seconds. No one can change Past not even predict the Future. Even Present will become our past after a second. Everyone is going to get mixed into the Earth and Nature will celebrate her victory over human like as happened in the past. So, World is full of joy live it in a every second of life.

## 2. "First Time"

When I stepped into this world of joy,
How much happiness did it bring to my family?
When I utter the first word,
How happy was family?
When I took my first step,
How surprisingly did they react?
When I did the first mistake of my life
How Calmly did they explain me?
When I went to school for the first time,
How worried they were?
When I was beaten for the first time,
How much pain they had to go through?
When I ride the cycle for the first time,
How scared they were?
When I lied to them for the first time,
How much it hurt them?
When I took my first step into the in-law's house,
How much they cried?
When I got pregnant for the first time,
How much elated they were?
When my body lies in the coffin for the first time
Now, none of them was there to cry for me, worry for me, take care of me,
PBut, those blessings of theirs (family) were always with me.

© Ipsa Swain.

## 3. "Because I'm Selfish"

Who am i?
Is there any existence of mine?
Why do my smile seems to be fake,
It doesn't have anymore shine.
Let it be,
Do you know what's my name
It's Selfish, you all named it,
Isn't its a good name?
After all it's given by you all.
I'm a happy man.
But not a happy soul in this joy of world.
Because, I'm Selfish.
I understand you,
But, no one ever understood me.
Because, I'm Selfish.
I care about you,
But, never care about Myself.
Beacuse, I'm Selfish.

You are always right,
And, I'm always wrong.
Beacuse, I'm Selfish.
Well, it suits me right.
Beacuse, It's me,
I born for Myself,
That makes me Selfish.
Because, Selfish me can make
'A world of joy'

# IPSITA

## 1. "The school : My World of joy"

Somehow in the age of crowd,
You taught me to stand like a stone in the ground.
From my intro to my ending,
You inspired me to not be someone...to be the only me.

Yes,sometimes my words,my behavior may bothered you..but
but but you know how much I care about you.

Remember,That tom and jerry fight..when you ran behind me to
catch me and win that race.

Hey,Did you Looked at that wall where we used to draw our
emotions by chalk!! Took a glance at that door,by which we
used to play hide and seek, and yes you were in winning team.
Remember that sadness when we got separated, that feelings
and emotions which can't be able to be shown.

Yes, I badly miss those days,when you and me were together in
that class and today also,I miss you as hell, but still I call you as
my best friend,why!!!! Just for your innocence and that atmost
care.
A school is the best place where there is a lot of emotions and
care. A school is a world where there is lot of joy and happiness.
And if your school time best friend, still with you , You are such
a Lucky person.
Because friendship is the best relationship ever.
© Ipsita mohapatra.

## ISHITA GARG

### 1. " I want to build "

A new world for everyone!

A world of love !

A world of joy !

A world of peace !

A world of hope !

A world of equality !

A world of wonders !

A world of happiness !

A world free of corona !

A world free of curruption !

A world full of fun !

A world of educated people !

If you also need,

this type of world,

take a step forward;

for your world,

and enjoy the life !!

# JASMINE PANDA

## 1. "The Beginning in world of joy"

With Love,
I believed two souls got united,
The day my life started!

In my mother's womb, my life started,
From that day, I think sadness departed!
My father took care each & every moment,
Love grew between them every second!

Smile and happiness on their way,
"Waiting to see me", they eagerly say!
I became their bond of togetherness,
Leaving all depression and stress!

The time came when I finally landed,
That was the moment most wanted!
Parents, tensed & happy, mixed feelings,
Taking energy from everybody's blessings!

The continuous cry on my little face,
Brought a smile on my parent's face!
Their love and happiness knew no bounds,
Both conversed with their eyes, no sound!

With Love,
I believed two souls got united,
The day my life started!

Forgetting all sorrows, staring at me,
An invisible contentment of feeling "we"!
Both were in pain, yet much satisfied,
For a new beginning, they were excited!

Looking around a new different place,
After nine months of complete darkness!
Blessed to come to the planet Earth,
Yes, it's difficult to realise my worth!

I, only I, yes, I, was their world of joy,
Everyone was staring at me like a toy!
Much care to nurture me the best,
Focus was on me, forgetting the rest!

Can never understand the sacrifice,
Of my parents and pay the price!
Can never feel the pain and endurance,
Throughout the journey, at a glance!

With Love,
I believed two souls got united,
The day my life started!

Taking me in their shivering hands,
A dream come true, a magic wand!
They feel heaven in their hands,

It seems happily, their souls dance!

To the supreme, to the Almighty,
Obligations to the utmost purity!
In search of words for gratitude,
Thanksgiving was the couple's attitude!

The same excitement every year,
For my most awaited birthday, so near!
Arrangements at its peak on my B'day,
Making me feel special on this day!

Let God bless my favourite couple,
To the two souls, very beautiful!
Let God bless their one and only child,
May she can become their pride!!!

With Love,
I believed two souls got united,
The day my life started!

©Jasmine Panda.

## JASMEET KAUR PASRICHA

### 1. "Joy : A Thirst To Grab or To Gain ? "

A world of joy is a world of ecstasy.
It is not in everyone 's destiny.
One may desire but do not aspire .
Not all are fortunate to be joyous.
Yearners relentless effort endure and attain.
Joy is not to grab but to gain.
Derive joy in your family.
Derive joy in serving mankind.
Derive joy in teaching deprived children.
Derive joy in the strength of honesty .
Derive joy in taking care of parents.
Respect, regard our elders, parents, seniors .
Acknowledge their contribution .
Joy is everywhere.
Be content to get joy
Do not contest to snatch joy.

## 2. "Portraying Joy : A* *Hypocrisy"

Joy and happiness do not define world of joy.
Joy lies inherently in all.
Very few look within.
Hypocrisy of joy is what people portray.
Sophistication is it's luring book mark.

Searching joy is not quintessential.
No one derives joy in serving aged parents.
Diseased and ailing.
Have nots and physically
Challenges are left unattended.

Instead utopia of joy is in pizza , kfc, swiggy.
Not knowing joy of a person released from a prison
Enlightenment is rare so is rare joy in day to day assignment.

© Jasmeet kaur pasricha.

# JENITHA.A

## 1. "The world of joy"

It was a city of peace ,
Where we see delightful gaze ,
Streets made of gold ,
Secrets are told .

Sudden light of glorious bright ,
Splendid Angel's dressed up white ,
Legend in eternal throne ,
Collection of gem in crown .

Sorrowful faces will flee ,
And rise the luminous glee ,
Mysterious place in high ,
Love and life beyond the sky .

When we are away from cris ,
It's a promise of eternal bliss ,
Ye,people are invited for foy ,
For it is the world of joy .

# JOY GRACE J

## 1. "JoyGalaxy"

I want to be the citizen of Joy,
Where I never need to cry,
Aspiring to taste the cup of bliss,
And to live with Zero percent stress,
Searching the country in every maps,
Simultaneously in every naps,
Googling the ways to get the visa,
Saving some money to settle in my utopia,
But wait....
The world is within me!!
My mind is the visa,
Self love is the flight,
I Just Forgot the Judgemental world!
I've Found my Joyful world!!
Ohh!!The World Of Joy
Is in the Galaxy within me...

## 2. "Saudade"

Longing to see you,
Yearning to hug you,
Dying to talk with you,
Starving to play with you ,
Craving to fight with you,
Hankering to laugh with you,
I'm searching words
To express my emotions,
But failing everytime
To control my tears,
I want to live with you,
Building castles in my dreams,
Your memories as the bricks,
But I never Imagined
That our Tryst is Paradise!!
I never imagined
I'll hold your hands
In the world of Joy!!
When Suadade seizes my thought
Your soul comfort me a lot....

© Joy Grace J.

# KALAMKAAR

## 1. "Intercaste relation"

The form of God is one, people have accepted God by dividing different religions.
Some have folded their hands and some have to go after praying.
World of joy if Someone remembers Allah.
Someone prays to Durga Mata to reduce their suffering.
Some people pray for their well being by fasting. This is world of joy if Some call upon Maa Durga to have darshan during Navratras.
Somebody goes to the mosque to pray.
There are temples of Mata to visit any caste. Some decorate the mosque when Ramadan comes.
Someone sings bhajans of the mother on the arrival of Navratri.
Sheer is made on the arrival of any Eid.
Kheer is made in some Teej festivals.
Some hug on Eid.
A lotus blooms by decorating someone's house in Diwali.
Some celebrate Holi, the festival of colors.
Some go to the homes of loved ones to give Iddi. Most of all go happily to meet loved ones every time Such is the festival of all religions.

©Kalamkaar

## 2. "Father : shelter of family"

Being in Dad's house makes the house safe.
If father is not at home then it feels incomplete.
If daddy is at home then the house seems complete.
Father takes care of everyone's safety.
Do not eat on your own and work hard for the family day and night.
Father becomes a family shield in difficult times.
Father fulfills the wishes of children in every situation.
Father works so hard that all the family members' needs are fulfilled.
Its world of joy At the festival when everyone smiled and celebrated the festival with happiness.
Its world of joy when Sweetness stay in family relations and let the bitterness go away.
Dad takes care of everyone's happiness.
Dad does nothing for himself but does everything for the family.
Those who think first for the family, not for themselves, are called fathers.

©Kalamkaar

## 3. "Quarantine 2020"

My quarantine life of 2020 was Hectic some time.
There was nothing to do,Everyone was bored at home.
I was also bored at home and could not understand what to do.
Writing became my love when I started to hear poet's namely kunal verma sir.
Hearing his poetry, words also started coming in my mind.
World of joy for me when i started writing,I used to write every day and its world of joy for me.
I made my account on your quote.
I used to write 25 poems, quote, shayari, sher in one day.
I didn't move from bed until I wrote on your quote.
Then I joined the writing community.
I used to participate in the Challenges and won the daily challenges.
Then I started participating in Anthologies.
I have worked in 870+ anthologies, and won 740+ certificates.
I found the artist inside me when I was quartine.
Became a writer in Quartin whom people know as Kalamkaar.

©Kalamkaar

# KAMLESH SINGH

## 1. "The voice of life"

It is difficult to define a happy life as different people associate happiness or joy with different things. In simpler words, when you are living in a happier space being grateful for everything there is in your life from relationships to materials — that's how a joyful life looks like to me.

Of course, the definition is open to multiple interpretations and frankly, that is exactly how it should be. After all, you shouldn't be following someone else's version of happiness. To all those reading this post, I would suggest you to pause for a while and think about your version of a joyful life. Imagine all the things that you need to be happy in life.

Let's take a look at the following seven secrets that could help you lead a happier and joyful life:
Start living with no regrets .One of the biggest reasons to your sad and empty life is your unfulfilled wishes and long-held resentments. Oftentimes, the saddest summary of life contains three descriptions: could have, might have, and should have. Start doing things that you always wanted to do, tick them off your bucket-list, and start living a life with no regrets

2. Start looking out for your passion

There is no joy like working day in and day out on something you're really passionate about. Knowing that you are dedicating your life to something purposeful is a hard feeling to be expressed in words. The thing about passion is that it makes your life both beautiful and worth living for.

### 3. Start spending some time in nature

People who feel a connection to nature and believe that nature is important to their lives are generally happier than those who don't. If you find it hard to believe this, there a scientific explanation to it as well. It says that when we observe the beauty of nature, our bodies produce lower levels of pro-inflammatory cytokines that makes our mood better.

### 4. Start looking after yourself

People often tend to forget that happiness starts from within. Nothing in this world can make you happier if you are not happier from inside. You must learn to look after yourself if you want to live a joyful life. The first step to do this is to start looking after your body.

### 5. Start giving back to the society

There is no such joy than knowing that you have added value in someone else's life — however small or big that contribution be. Giving back to the society not only helps us to be generous and benevolent but also gives us a sense of purpose. It also makes

you happier knowing that once you did something for others not just for yourself.

"At the end of the day it's not about what you have or what you've accomplished... It's all about who you've lifted up, who you've made better. It's about what you'v

## 6. Start investing in your growth

The one thing that is strikingly similar among all successful folks is that they are damn serious about their growth — mental, physical, intellectual, and financial. Knowing the very fact that you are becoming better with every passing day helps you enjoy your life even more.

You can start reading books, blogs, watch inspirational videos, read interviews, listen to podcasts to stimulate your growth. All these habits and actions will have a profound effect on your overall well-being and happiness in world of joy.

© Kamlesh Singh.

# KAMU PILLAI

## 1. "Life's calling"

The sun rises with hope To brighten the world. The people waken with a desire To achieve something worth it. Creatures discern the realm Of grace & compassion. Occasionally few arouse with an acceptable motive And rare with miserable constraint. Though we seek and aspire barely to disseminate (Anyhow to put across the day). just to behold the end that what it precisely appear within. Nobody got uptight with what the Situation is all about. Folks go in search of par hegemony Not efficient to comprehend their inferiority. Stop discovering a solution rather than convince yourself that you can face everything on your own. Feel gracious in a hard situation And be more fascinated while getting at outcomes. Let's not destroy putting yourself into the world of joy; live it, it's yours

## 2. "The desire in world of joy "

Immortal are those who rely on
There's nothing that lasts forever.
Some undervalued & rare discerned To heal,
you must stay out of what shattered you the most.
You suffer then you thrive through,
The exact someone will compel
you to fall in love with yourself too.

©Kamu Pillai .

# KAVITHA

## 1. "Happiness overloaded"

We were drenched, dress was dirty, full of dust and sand on our head and body with no worries. I heard a voice " Come soon you have home works to do" which was most familiar.
It was my mom.I had rushed to home.
In the middle of meeting break my memories said" It was the world of joy" but it cannot be continued as you are grown-up now.

## 2. "World of joy"

He was crying infront of the door, but they refused to allow him in. People around him tried convincing him from shedding tears, but they couldn't.

Suddenly he smiled at the door, doctor came out and said " Congratulations 'She' is born".

©Kavitha

# K. ESWARI

## 1. "Annoyings of brother"

Second king of every girl !
The person who loves us more
But never shows infront of us !
Most of the times they proved
Their immortal love through anger !
One and only locker of
All our secrets !
The person who enjoy our
Pretty waggeries and pretend
Infront of us !
All the times he finds our mistakes
And reveals it infront of us
During the silly fights !
Sleeping in his lap is heaven !
But he never gift it for us!
The one and only person who annoys us and never leave
Us allone is our awsome brother!
Every day "In the world of joy" !

# KHUSHI YADAV

## 1. "The Dark Night"

An endless dark ocean in the sky
And sparkling stars as the waves
I look up as a sparkle falls down
Upon the painful lands
My eyes are closed as tightly as the fists of someone holding onto
A memory they can't let go of
I make a wish and the gates to another World dawn upon me
As my steps tread into the world
Sorrow seems to be long forgotten
And the emptiness in me makes way for something fulfilling
At last I have found my way into the world of joy
I look back and the dark ocean
Merges with the land beneath
And all that's left is the sparkling stars

## 2. "It's With You"

Deep down in the woods,
There's a path not known to many
It leads you to another world
A world desired by many
But conquered by few
The world of joy, where no sorrow lasts
And no grief can overtake
Where the people know only happiness
And the only sound is the laughter
Where the smiles are simple
And the trees bloom with joy
Where no emptiness can ever creep into the hearts of people
For they are full with joy
I will let you on a little secret which will help you find the place
Look into your heart and travel through your mind
And one day you will reach this world of joy

© Khushi Yadav.

## 3. "The Street"

Walking along a strange street
I stumbled upon a path I knew was familiar
And even though I had somewhere to be
I couldn't bring myself to leave this street
So I walked along the gigglying homes
And before I knew it
I came along my very own home
My childhood home it seems
Buried in memories but never forgotten
And as I took a step forward
I looked upon my favourite tree
My swing still hanging from it's old branches
It looked as if just yesterday I was high up in the sky
And as a smile grew upon my face
I realised this was my world of joy

© Khushi Yadav.

# KOMAL JANARDAN SRIVASTAV

## 1. "A world of dream"

When I start writing,
happiness I feel deep inside!
To me,
the world of joy is like,
writing a story,
poem and micro tale.

For me,
I create my world,
different from society.

Where I am superior.
A world of my dream.

I am working hard,
to make it possible.

A dream of world,
where I am flying;
ahead of the whole world,

Where, I am completing all my wishes.
Untill it comes true,
let's work hard,
to complete the dream.
© Komal Janardan Srivastav

# K. PREETHI

## 1. "STAGES OF JOY"

Childhood is a bliss
Full package of joy
It is seeded as innocence
Buds as ignorance
Blooms as discovery
Happy in playing toys
Blushes on noticing chocolates
Refreshes in tasting ice-creams
Revolves in their own world
Expert of unknown language
Heavenly bliss on hearing
Broken words,lingering voice
Newly born flowers
Blushes of godly fragrance,
Teen's world enveloped as cocoons
Future blaster as beautiful butterflies
A half-grown moustache
A shyness of eye-sight
Hours of leisure
It's their pleasure
At an sight of an girl
Eyes glitter as pearl
Hesitates to speak
Nervous at peak
Trembling hands

World Of Joy

Shivering words
Uncontrollable heart beats
Unexpressed emotions
Bind as treble joy,
An eye-sight of his love.
Encloses whole universe
Overwhelming imaginations
Trials of cinematic proposals
Unexpected birthday gifts
Idioms of sentence
Identity of FLAMES
Execution of master plans
Fantastic joy of thriller,
Adult's footprints in college
Roaring bike entry as hero
Excels in academics as zero
Imagine their image as Don's
Well-managed as Mahan's
Falling in love with pretty girls
Finally pity boy's
Calls of pick-ups
Ends with break-ups
Will of enjoy
Neglects bye-bye
Pleasure of theatre and fun
Altogether,stops with pun
Academics and career
Flourishes with arrears
Ultimately, he realizes his stage
Blabbers and acquires vision of sage
Middle age, an experience
Strictness of father

Will be understood later
Advice of mother
Will give vision brighter
Unwanted friendship
Hated slower
An gift of Marriage
Opens gradual petals
As unknown surprise
Post of caring husband
Promotion of responsible father
Burden's his shoulders
Bends as ladders
Burns as candles
Melts as sweats
Good growth of children
Boosts to run! run!
Victory of children
Makes proud to be then
As a father, watches with trick
As kite, adjusts the thread
To concentrate on life's war
To stamp the state of star,
An old-age is an nostalgic of infancy
Eyes dims its sight
Ears lose its sound
Words blabber as child
Strength decreases as mild
Real power rejuvenates
When an young hand reunites
Steps of walks, reduces shorter
Crawls as child later
Ends with death bitter,

## World Of Joy

Let's live with joy
Spread wings as butterflies
Joy changes on occasions
It depends on perspectives
Make our own "WORLD OF JOY"
An hidden gift concealed in hands
Live our life
Achieve our goal
Address our own
Applause of joy
Abundance of blessings
Admit thanks to God.

## LELSEY MAGWAZA

### 1. "Seasons Change"

Every living creature has a season to bloom,
Everything on earth works with time,
The time you've chosen subconsciously to bloom in "world of joy",
You might be fighting your battles but not seeing where you are going and how you'll get there, but keep faith within your heart and know that I am God,
Some trees go on all year long with green leaves,
That's the depth of how deep their roots go and reach for refined wells,
Some trees may have lost all their leaves during winter seasons,
Yet they are aware that to bloom again they'd have to let go of those leaves and remain naked and I the God of all creations will restore what has been broken,
Much better than it was previously,

There are seasons that seem to take away everything we love and have us believe that we are being punished, but in actual truth we are as a catapillar becoming a butterfly,
Every living creature presumes transformation,
It's pretty typical with a human nature,
You presume transformation within before it reveals without,
Even if you don't show it, it will manifest itself,

Take for instance a child,

## World Of Joy

A child is an observation, adverntous being, likes no limitation
and simply IS the purest form of a spirit,
Playing, Laughing, crying and exploring new tools to play with,
Simply having no worry at all,
Yet as the child presumes growth,
All those tools that once mattered are dropped down gently
and a new course of life has been taken, thus letting go for
transformation to occur,
There after we see a functional and reasoning being also
questions the existence and the average population's behavior,
Thus now choosing to become and filtering what not to become
through guidance of our creator,
Soon the child sees that there's more to life than that meets the
eyes now opening the  third eye to be the mediator,
So seated under trees discovering the fruits within and planting
new seeds that'll beautifully bloom later,
All the experiences placed before that being is a reminder
because in truth what's hurting you now will soon not matter,
For all your blessings will be brought by heaven in me on a silver
platter,
From there on things will be better,
And thus we live in the world of Joy, peace and love forever.

© Lesley Magwaza.

## 2. "Unfolding the Folders"

I see the strains,
The consticted veins,
The rail road trains,
Chuckling the labour pains,

I am born of this world but not from this world,
I am thee Alpha and Omega,
The devil is the liar,
The deceiver who decieves through Delilah,
The journey started never ended until I become me,
Thy kingdom come in me,
Thy will be done in me,
See,
Without thee,
I don't see me,
You see me, me
Me I'm a harbinger,
God's messenger,
A truth teller,
More like a fortune teller,
See that other fellow,
He said there ain't no God,
I told him I'm a proof of God,
Something he can't even afford,
I'm priceless if you agree with me let me see you nod,
My words are sparkling and highly blessed like iron specre and rod,
Those who don't know the truth as I speak will get bored,

Anyway let's get to the point,

## World Of Joy

We ovulate to make more of us,
We are more than what an Egyptian pyramids could encampus,
More than what Bible scriptures preach of us,
The limitless beings occupying the "world of joy",
We surpassed the illusion of time and space in between us,
We are transforming to the higher dimensions that are prime and optimal,
Eradicating false beliefs and pseudo science that claims to have made us who we are,
We come a long way but not too far,
The piece of higher self shared to you in the moment of now is yet a piece of an ice berg,
There's more to you and I than what meets the eye,
It shall be revealed to you as soon as you open your third eye.

© Lesley Magwaza.

## 3. "Here and Now"

Breath to me life, I won't know how to live when you aren't here with me, now give to light I won't know where's the without here and, now bring peace to me now I wish to live and love harmoniously, and Here's what's going to up lift my life with you to live deliberately, peacefully and joyfully in "world of joy".

© Lesley Magwaza.

# MAMTA

## 1. "World of Joy"

Somewhere far
From the crowd
I m living in the
World of Joy
Having fantacies in
My visionary world.

Looking for things
In my surroundings
That give me happiness
For a while and end up with smile.

Dreaming of what I could be
I pray and trying hard to reach out.

Spreading my wings and
Learning how to fly.

And sometimes I just allowed myself liberty
Of releasing my emotions.

## 2. "Goosebumps"

Thinking about the moment of joy
Where I will just goosebumps
And literally feeling same yet
In the way I will
I m able to feel
While I'm living
In the world of Joy.
Having my cup of tea
With the book to read.
It will mesmerize my heart
And that is just a bliss
Of the world.

© Mamta.

## 3. "Hidden"

Everyone have just
Soft corner
Inside of their depth
Where they will nurture
And heal the soul
Like a dazzling bloom
For your own spot.
A pious soul is just
Hidden inside the depth
You just have to unleash
And act like as bright spot.
It will come from the
Feeling of the world ofjoy while
You feel it from inner self.

© Mamta.

# MANSHA GOYAL

## 1. "The Day We Met"

I never knew that someone would be so mature.
Someone would be so pure by heart
Someone who can adore my immaturity.
Someone who can make me laugh by cracking silly jokes.

Someone who doesn't let me cry.
Someone who doesn't let me feel low.
Someone available for me 24/7.
Someone would become my umbrella in rain.
Someone would be light in the dark.

Who just not only corrects me but tells my mistakes.
Who always respects me and my decision.
Who has not to care for her lady but also every lady?
Innocence in eyes, a kid in the heart.
How can someone be so positive by mind?

Over some time
I get to know about a real gentleman.
Thank you for making my life changed
And lastly
I still remember the day we met. ( World of Joy )

## 2. "Silence Screams"

Water from eyes
Is the most silence scream
It breaks into pieces
When heart fails
Soul screams
And
Silence screams more louder
No happiness can heal this pain
When one soul ditaches itself from other
Everything obscured
And life gets over ( World of Joy ).

## 3. "A disable Girl"

A girl whose face was eaten by acid was so innocent calmed and sweet who love to sleep in nature's lap once who had wish to conquer the world once who want to fly high and high , today can't face herself due to this cruel world whom make her soft heart' an evil's heart because of her face. World make her realised that she can't live her life happily.. and makes her positivity to let turn into a negative one .... Not only society but her own family members makes her feel low... But she still have a hope to overcome such huddles and let this disability be her ability to achieve goals to be known by the people. Never underestimate someone by their looks just because you will be not known by your complexion you will be known by your work and struggle in the World of Joy.

© Mansha Goyal.

# MATANGI PRIYA MURALIDHARAN

## 1. "Glass Heart"

This glass heart
Isn't fragile as it has to be,
Nor melting with the burning fire within.
It shattered into pieces, many a times in "world of joy"
But still withhold itself
Just to hold it's loved ones.
Not once did those broken pieces
Stab nor pierce others knowingly
But bleeds itself in pain
With a loving attitude.
A glass heart
With iron fillings.

## 2. "Angel"

Fall like a feather
Silently
Defying gravity
With style.
That confuses the onlookers,
Whether it's a fall or a flight.
May the with of opportunities
Will rise the flight in the midway,
That roars high.
If it's a fall a soft non harming lesson.
Whether it's a flight or fall
The Angel is always an Angel in world of joy.
Defining the World of Joy
To the content of hearts.

©Ipraymadhi

## 3. "Young Mind"

Once upon a midnight
Mind didn't wander
And
Heart was happily satisfied.
Nothing that matters now,
But then it was all that mattered.
It was a fairytale,
Not the worries of tomorrow,
Nor the fears of the past,
But the strength of that young mind
Ready to face anything.
Believing in self that nothing is impossible to do.
Yes!
That little version is what made us,
Us in the present.
But it's lost as a once upon time,
Just cause some forgot what really matters
That's The World of Joy
That we created for ourself.

©Ipraymadhi .

# M.MARIA HELEN JANOBA

## 1. "To My Love"

The intervallic joy
of small happenings
is upon an individual...
Remember the world of joy?
Let's find a room in the heavenly earth
with a window onto elms
face the sunlight,
a cafe with polished cups,
darling drug they call it,
may our bed be decorated
with fresh tulips
and glinting thyme,
all herbs in due season
folded on the sheets
fit for the conjugation of joy

## 2. "Mother Land"

Earth!
Welcome her seasons wealth,
Every bough is, like a lyre,
Answering to the wind's low singing
Sweet as bells from heaven!
The sounds from the fountain,
Softer bloom upon the flower
The buds are shrinking with shy
Yeah!
The world of joy
Even a single creature enjoys its presence
On the mother earth!

©M.Maria Helen Janoba.

## 3. "Bliss"

Woke up with hope
The ray of sunshine gives energy to life
Morning alarm feels like the heavenly bell
The chirping of birds
Like melodies of life
The wind is blowing its gentle touch
Droplets on the grasses are like diamonds
Find solace at your arms
It feels like
The world of joy
With Nature and with YOU
Both bestow me delight...

©M.Maria Helen Janoba.

# M.CATHRIN JENIPHER

## 1. " A Mysterious Trip"

Once there lived two Angels in heaven named Christina and Joyce who always loves to make others happy in heaven.One day Christina and Joyce wished to visit the world and decided to land in the Disney World to make their trip a funfilled one.Once they reached the Disney World,Micky and his friends welcomed them with a great feast and presented lots of gifts to them as a token of love.The Angels enjoyed the feast with lots of happiness and spent their time with joy by singing ,dancing etc...The next day morning Angels decided to have a look on the entire Disney World.Angels on looking the palace noticed some Micky's playing with their friends.On seeing that ,Angels also wished to make lots of friends for them.They also wished to make their, trip to world an unforgettable one.As per their wish they decided to go to Jammu and Kashmir.The angels also shared this idea with a Micky.The Micky also agreed to it.Few days later Micky to surprise the Angels Christina and Joyce decided to bring Kitty to his palace to create more joyful moments.While the Angels Christina and Joyce were in garden playing musical instruments with a marvelous tone Micky made kitty to stand in the garden.The Angels ,was surprised to see the Kitty there standing between the two rose plants. The Angels and Kitty became friends and shared many secrets.The kitty presented them a beautiful Magic stick which is a rare piece for Angels.The Angels also liked the Kitty more and they often started to danced with her.One day while having their breakfast in the dinning table Angels noticed that Kitty was upset.The Angels remembered the Kitty's secret where she told about her friend Rose who is no more.And ,it was a day for Rose which is her birthday.So,Kitty was upset on her rememberance and Angels tried to make her happy by making her laugh by sharing funny incidents.The Angels who loves to go around the world decided to take Micky and Kitty along with them to make their trip more special.The Micky and Kitty also agreed to take the trip .As soon as the planning session over Kitty and Micky were busy in designing their costume for the trip.The next morning the two Angels,Micky and Kitty started their trip by a car and enjoyed a lot along their way.Finally,in the middle of the way to Jammu and Kashmir they saw Dora and Buji standing along with their bag and map.They were also struggling to go further.The Angels,Micky and Kitty on seeing them decided to help them.Finally the angels welcomed Dora and Buji to join their trip.As soon as they started their trip further ,they noticed Dora was little upset that Jack the cunning fox has stollen her beautiful ribbon which was presented by her mom

the angels and the friends in the car convinced her and went in search of fox to get her ribbon back.The Kitty who is sitting in the window seat was very curious to find the Jack.The Kitty ,in the midway started shouting,"The Jack is there".Suddenly they stopped their car and the angels went near the fox and he is very busy in playing candy crush game and slowly turned back on hearing the Angel's voice.The Angels asked Jack about Dora's ribbon and also adviced him not to steal anymore in future.Jack agreeing it , asked the Angel's that he is also wished to join their trip.The Angels also agreed to it and took Jack along with them.As soon as getting inside the car Jack returned the ribbon to Dora and apologized for stealing it.He also promised that he won't do the same in future.Thus,they again resumed their trip with lot of happiness and joy by singing,playing games etc..Finally,after reaching Kashmir Angels,Kitty,Jack,Micky,Dora and Buji had a great funny trek and they were welcomed by a troop of kids who were a big fan of them and they also gave them a great party.The party ended with lot of happiness and joy and the whole team containg kids,kitty,Jack,Micky,Angels,Dora and Buji danced ,sang a song and shared gifts.Thus ,the trip also ended with lots of golden memories.The whole trip became a most beautiful trip by two Angels who always loved to make others happy.The Angels as per their wish they got many friends ,who made their trip a really awesome and joyful.

"The beauty can always seen in making others happy,
Making others happy brings joy in one's heart,
One's heart can make the entire world happy
Thus,the world of joy becomes the whole..."

©M.Cathrin Jenipher.

# M. DHANALAXMI MANDIRAM

## 1. "World of Joy"

Everytime, we can't be happy,
But I wish, why I can't be like a Mr.Bean,
Who is happy all the time,
Enjoying every phrase of his life.
Every little thing, I used to feel happy about it,
Swing in the air,
Feeling the nature,
Enjoying with colleagues,
It's always about the joyful moments.
At recent times, we are enjoying,
By seeing funny videos,
But forgets to enjoy the present with family.
On this lockdown,
Relaxing every minute,
By eating -sleeping routine,
This is what my world of joy exists.
If you want to enjoy everytime, try not to expect anything,
But silently living a happy life in imagination.

## 2. " Short story - Parent's Love"

I was happily living with my parents, when I grew up, I started to lose my love on my parents. I used to hate them everytime and whenever they scold me and I used to hate even more. I started to live alone at my home. When I came to know that one of my friend doesn't have father and she loved him so much. But felt unlucky for not having father and I'm having but not respecting them. I started to realise my parents. A day comes when I wish something to do and my mom's doesn't like it but I disrespectfully does that work ,she accompany me. And my dad, when I don't know how to drive, he said,"I'm there, no need to worry" that is what made me boostup to love more. And when they talk about my marriage, I feel low of being that after days, I will become guest of my own house. Even the thought of this would hold a tears in my eyes that I will lose some day. So i started to enjoy with them, by using the lockdown phrase. They became my world of joy.

© M. Dhanalaxmi Mandiram.

## 3. "Brother's Love -poem"

On golden days, I was happily enjoying my life with my blood,
Playing, laughing and communicating with each other.
He had a desire to call him as my brother,
But before completing his wish, he left me.
Galvanize that my blood left from my body and I became a snowman.
His memories will be constant.
You will be there at my hardships,
Sailing with me, walking with me as my footprint.

My family is my world of joy.

© M. Dhanalaxmi Mandiram.

## MOHAMMED NIYAZ

### 1. *"Treasure Of Happiness"*

Worth of time that's been now and whole.
To the celebrations of victory within the core.

The excitement has changed even moods.
Making up the best of odds stood.

Those who chanced to revenge their mistakes.
Will now being happy to see the flakes.

"The world of joy" is another planet for us.
When creations has created something off fuss.

Nobody has been in a proportion of guess.
Un til the evidence got clicked till mess.

You know what if means of merrier come.
To the grounds of oceanic home.

Lies of the truth is needed to be added.
To the needful of additions headed.

The sole surrounds get name tag of emotions less.
When you discover the scenario through "treasure of happiness".
©Mohammed Niyaz.

# M. SURIYAA

## 1. *"Barren Allure"*

The lush forest of corals:
Manifests a world of joy,
Habitat of thousand shades,
Canvas of the heavenly brush,
Canopied by the water so pure;
With the solid hue of aquamarine,
A little blue lightly tinged.
Ebullient portrait of numerous;
Life forms not wholly encapsulated,
Sadly a sedimentation,
Of the broken down adamantine destroyer,
From the disappeared dumped garbage,
Already in combat with the living things
Magnanimous beauty eroded of age.

# MUSKAN PATTNAIK

## 1. "Real god in this world of joy"

Even a child also has in his book -Whom do we go when we are sick? Who treat us with love, passion ,care,affection?It's Doctors ,Nurses and the whole of health staffs.They are really a boon to us .They are not just lucky to have us as their patients but we are much luckier than them to have them as our health staff.Have always listen to one thing and do also believe that God can't talk but can see the world with one eye sight .So, you don't stop doing your deeds,keep on doing ,one or the other day you will be the winner!. You have never thought this as your duty ,rather your passion. Your godly service can't be expressed in words. Some say that don't go to doctor because if a person is all well since years and months and days then how suddenly?? And for which family gains popularity .But do they ever realise that those who have felt the touch of Doctors with love, care and those advisable advice for patients is the best feeling in the world .They have never made us realise that we are alone and if sometimes our family members don't stand for the us ,they stand as a pillar of hope ,light. Those distractions to child while taking injection ,those delightful moments of fun,laughter,happiness are the best. Sometimes, we lose our confidence and will power but seeing you ,we gear up ourselves because you are the one who is the most important and serious person at that time .We have heard this proverb-'an Apple a day keeps a doctor away '.So we come to know that everyday if we eat one Apple we won't fall sick.Now ,if we don't fall sick or get any injury then how can we get to the meaning of Doctors and health staffs ?Their work?So ,we should remain fit and healthy. That's doesn't mean that diseases won't catch us .If there is a body ,then diseases are to be there. So,we need to be careful!!

© Muskan Pattnaik.

# NAMITA RUPANI

## 1. *"Trip to beas..."*

It's Place close to my soul
This place is My world of joy
Where I love to reside
It's in Punjab near Amritsar
The place full of heaven and peace
The place is blessed by our guruji
Believe me when I say heaven
No other place can be as beautiful as beas
Do sewa there attending Satsang
Is the best thing one can explore for peace
Lakhs of people come from all over the world
Radhasoami is chanted all over
It's a place where all people are equal
Be it poor or rich, whichever caste whichever religion everybody is served equally.
Not only adults but kids all enjoy and get blessing and do Sewa at beas
It a city filled with love care peace allover
One must visit this place called beas that is my world of joy.....

## 2. *"The arms close to my* *heart..."*

Parent's arms where we all get peace
No one can replace their arms
Their caring love responsibility doesn't no matter how big we grow
For these arms are world of joy for every child
Parents took us through all the steps of our life
From being kid to adult their love remains constant
We can't measure their love as it's infinite
Being a kid we should bestow same love and care when they grow old
It's not giving and take but taking care of parents is the biggest sin you can ever do in your life
Be it any situation don't ever leave their hands
Hold their hands for a lifetime you will find a world of joy all over.

© Namita Rupani.

## 3. "True relationships still exists...."

A true relationship just need trust understanding loving bond with each other
Remember we clap from both hands it's the same in a relationship give your best you will get the best in return
It's just balance of families balance of responsibility and being honest with your partner
If you carry your relationship in right manner nothing can break it
Remember ball is always in your court
Give time to your relationships , be freinds first your love will bloom and your world of joy will earge you to live happily ever after.

© Namita Rupani.

# NAURISH ALAM

## 1. *"Beauty of Self note"*

Sometimes I want to cry
But is it okay
To be an unreasonable tears
Which is not yours but other creation
Surrounded between fake friendship
And still smile and act like you don't care. BUt you care deep down its hurt like a hell and it's a world of joy
This thing need to change ,when you become heartless , nothing effected n bothered you
And I want this but this too caring n innocent heart is dumb .
Although every second ,I force myself to remember that everybody comes in your life to Change your life and teaches a lesson and later I sleep or we can say escape form dull nights and make wish that next morning everything will fine and after dark night ,bright morning waiting for me with blessings of God and something better from my rotten thoughts .

© Naurish Alam.

## 2. "Music"

Why ,She loves the classic voice
Many ears wait for a classic voice
Deep and love
Seen in each words
Still feels the aroma in rewind
In the twentieth century of rocking time
She loves the classic voice
I might wrong many times
But I think it's a last time a world of joy
Try once the classic voice
Heaven comes to hear this
Anxiety and depression goes away
Healing droughts in few minutes
Just magic happens for minutes
She loves the classic music

© Naurish Alam.

## 3. "I met another heartbreak"

I met another heartbreak
This winter night too long to awaken
Pillows and tears mix like painting
Heart shattered in little pieces
I wish ,I had dream of world of joy

Beloved changed into stranger once again
Again,Destiny played a game
Again ,I met with a heartbreak
Again,I met eyes and lid

© Naurish Alam.

## NAVEEN BHARDWAJ

### 1. "Love"

What it's feels like if you ask someone what is love;
Some tells it's a feeling that can't expressed in words;
Do you believe love at first sight;
I bet you don't ; it's a significant bonding between the two;
And finally we meet someone who look at us in the same way;
They speaks , feels with us at the same rhythm;
We feels the chemistry between the two;
It started from a nice talk to a endless talk;
The force of our love was too strong to resist;
For some love is kind of confusing thing to hold;
It's a one letter word ; that is more explicit to call;
It can be exist in many things in this "world of joy";
Like erotic to feeling , fun to adventure;
Many people define love in their own words;
Love is not static ; it can be found in many form;
From one time you love them and the other you don't;
But it's a feeling that can't expressed in words;
While you say I am falling for you;
You are just falling for their body not with their inner form;
It's not a obsession ; it's not a dying for each other;
It's a give and take things that works for each other;

## 2. "World of joy"

When I feel like I am not improving;
I look in the mirror and see my old picture of me;
Mirror are mostly used to intended ;
That can tell you who is the best looking person in this world;
We usually hide ourself from reality;
Hiding in the crowd where no one sees us;
People say it didn't show us out true image;
It doesnt mean it show wrong reality of mine;
What if a mirror you using everyday lying to you;
Our true beauty lie within you;
Not in mirror , not in camera or gadgets;
Think about it when you smile or cry you need mirror or not;
But then also we live in this dillussional world;
Thinking all these problem we facing today cannot hide in mirror;
The changes comes within you;

©Naveen Bhardwaj

## 3. "Mirror"

When I feel like I am not improving;
I look in the mirror and see my old picture of me;
Mirror are mostly used to intended ;
That can tell you who is the best looking person in this world;
We usually hide ourself from reality;
Hiding in the crowd where no one sees us;
People say it didn't show us out true image;
It doesnt mean it show wrong reality of mine;
What if a mirror you using everyday lying to you;
Our true beauty lie within you;
Not in mirror , not in camera or gadgets;
Think about it when you smile or cry you need mirror or not;
But then also we live in this dillussional "world of joy";
Thinking all these problem we facing today cannot hide in mirror;
The changes comes within you;

©Naveen Bhardwaj

## 4. "Imperfection"

I was the person who never talk to anyone untill I meet you;
Relationship are not perfect ; but those are people, who turn the relationship into a tale of riddles;
From introvert to a jolly person , you are someone who makes me feels different from others in this entire "world of joy";
For a perfect relationship you first need a so called "perfect" person in life;
Who will project a imperfect relationship on anyone;
Nobody is perfect we need to understand this quote;
Accept the person for who he is not what he might in past;
Never think like you are perfect , just take it easy;
Be yourself and don't get fed up with small things;

©Naveen Bhardwaj

## NEETI YADAV

### 1. The world of joy now

My world of joy is now myself
I am tired with people
I now crave self love
and some sweet.
You needn't worry
about my pain.
Like sweets,
medicines are also mine
Leave me alone
to live with me

## NIK RAJPUT

### 1. "How to tell...?"

What is your life without telling you how?
How to tell die a new death every day in this "world of joy"

Some dreams remain unfulfilled in life
How to tell tales of an incomplete story.

There is no other cure for this pain,
How can we tell this to the innocent heart?

All busy in their own life
To whom have we told our condition?

We would have saved ourselves from false laughter
But who can tell the sadness of the face?

We have a flood of tears in our eyes;
How to make your dreams a reality....

© Nik Rajput.

## 2. "How to live without you?"

You feel incomplete in the bin.
The "world of joy" feel incomplete without you...
And even the house seems incomplete without you.

like a deer
The whole forest seems incomplete.

like without water
Life seems incomplete.

like clouds open
The sky seems incomplete.

like a blank without words
The paper seems incomplete.

like without flowers
The garden seems incomplete.

like a dream without sleep
It seems incomplete.

like without your life
We feel incomplete.

like ours without a shadow
The existence seems incomplete.

© Nik Rajput.

## 3. "Between us..."

The love is still there between the two of us.
There are untold things between the two of us.

Few days in our relationship
There is a rift between the two of us.

He will be away from us but in the heart....
There is a concern between the two of us.

Don't know why the fight happened but...
The love is still there between the two of us.

The fight was with eyes, I don't know
How did words happen between us?

We were both in our relationship before...
Now there is an agreement between the two of us.

I don't know why hate today
There is a wall built between us today.

Wet teachings will remain in love but...
Love exists between the two of us in this "world of joy".

© Nik Rajput.

# NOOR TABASSUM

## 1. "BEWARE HOW YOU REACT TO THE SITIUATION IN WORLD OF JOY"

It was a sweltering day when I stood waiting for the bus to reach my home from college. I was exhausted after a long day at college. My mood was terrible. Amidst all this, I was disturbed by someone mending with my veil, but I snubbed it. I had turned my face towards the other side. I did not want to look back, so I just ignored it. But I lost my patience when his audacity increased, and he touched my shoulder. I turned around and slapped tight on his face. When I saw him, he was a boy who was 18 years old, and tears had filled in his eyes. He was shivering with fear at an unexpected slap. He looked healthy and was handsome to look at. He started saying, “Bad aunty, bad aunty.” His words enraged me more. I thought, how dare he call me aunty when I may be almost of the same age.

I felt like slapping him again, but I controlled my emotions and stared hard at him. His mother rushed to his rescue, screaming that he was innocent. She said that he tried to lift my veil, sweeping on the floor, and trying to place it on my shoulder. She said that her son had no intention of teasing or touching me. He was as pure as snow in his objectives as he had a five-year old’s mental ability. That boy was a mentally challenged person. He hid behind his mom when I looked at him. His

mother went on, saying that he was unwell. He did not intend any misconduct by touching me. Her voice had the pain which filled me with intense repentance. Those crying eyes and shivering voice made me tremendously appalling. I wished the earth opened, and I got buried in it. My eyes were also filled with painful tears. When finally, I looked up to ask for forgiveness, they had vanished. I searched for them everywhere but could not trace them. I can never forget this incident.
I pondered on my action and was furious with myself for the conduct I did. I wondered who was mentally ill? According to me, I was sicker than him for reacting to the situation without analyzing it. Our frustrations and anger should not rule us. Our emotional clashes should be under our control. From then on, I learned my lesson. I understood that we should be careful about our actions. First, be sure about the situation and then react. Just because we consider ourselves normal does not mean we respond the way we like. And never be judgmental about everybody. Every person is different from one another. This world is filled with joy, please enjoy it sensibly.

## 2. "Corona"

Oh, tyrant corona, is your tummy still hungry,
When will you serene from your furious, angry,
How huge is your vicious tummy?
That you are devouring everyone irrespective of baby or mummy.

Thousands have drowned in you,
Millions are crying because of you,
Numerous have lost their jobs because of you,
Businesses have conked since you started to chew.

The world has been shadowed with black clouds of sorrow,
People crying and wailing injured by your arrow,
Because of the prevailing lockdown, people are hiding in the burrow,
Hungry stomachs are grunting loud because of the unemployment that has followed.

So tiny virus you are, yet so powerful,
But enough is enough; this is very hurtful,
Let life become again beautiful and colourful,
Fed up with attaining people's funerals.

Oh God, please bring back the world of joy,
Where every second is worth living and filled with hay.

© Noor Tabassum

# P.DHANSHA

## 1. "My home is my world of joy"

A home is a place where,
togetherness of love resides;
joyous memories are generated and
laughter never ending.

It is my place of confidence,
where I feel loved, appreciated and safe;
It is my place where
I start from,
where I pour out my emotions;
It is the spot, where my
expressions of tenderness gush out,
without any sensation of awkwardness;
It is the spot of earth admirably blest,
where my father's benevolence is higher than the mountains;
my mother's morality is deeper than the sea;
they are my wings for my dreams;
It is my real comfort zone;
And it is the only place where I feel my heart is connected with it.
And my home is my world of joy...

# PRATEEK ROHATGI

## 1. "Your dreams"

The dreams that come to mind
Not while sleeping but those which do not let to sleep.
Chasing them all the day long
And then you just one day come across
Chasing those dreams whole day
Whole week, whole month, whole year and whole life
To the point where you wanted to be in your life
And when you see behind
You get to see a world of joy
Waiting for you to the place where you wanted
But from a place where you started chasing your dream.

## 2. "World of child"

For every child his world of joy
Is his father who brings his favourite toy
Or his mother who fights with the world for her child.
His brother who helps and supports him from every trouble of life
Or his sister who solves his every problem in no time.
His friends who remain with him and solves all his problems.
Or his wife who lets him stand and fight with the problem himself.
The world of joy is bound to the child from his birth.
And remains with him to the end of his life.
But the only thing needed is the need to understand
And look inside the heart.

©Prateek Rohatgi.

## 3. "The world"

In this world of joy and sorry
People rotate on a track
Where they are indefinite about their needs
Or I say about their goals
The kiosk and confusion in their mind
Leads to the pitfall with the blowing wind
Which will just flow it and have no end
The people who are definite with their goals
And work steadily have the definite end.
But the end is a unique end
And a happy end.

## PRIYA MANCHANDA

### 1. "Life phases"

Life is like as easy as creating pout,
So don't ever shout,
Do you even know how much you are bold and loud,
Do something good,
And make your's parents proud,
In the world full of joy,
Be someone's spouse,
Do best things and create some crowd,
Make yourself at number one,
Do chill and fun,
When no-one is around,
Be free, don't bound,
Stay, when good souls are around,
Believe in karma, as it goes round and round,
Sometimes life create mess,
It may appear cloud,
Or maybe you got wound,
The right path you have to found,
Trust the timing of God,
Isn't it's good sound??

## 2. "World of joy and pain"

In the world of joy and pain,
Like is running like train,
Don't be insane,
Feel the wonderful rain,
Just imagine in your brain,
You're in the arms of your main,
Traveling in a plain,
On the way to Spain,
Binding the partner in a strong chain,
Only love from you I want to gain,
All the things now I explained,
Now, it's your duty to arrange,
In the world full of joy and pain,
You always stay same...!!

#Your's Babygirl!!

©Priya Manchanda.

## 3. "Joy"

Make your little world full with joy. Cherish every moment. Celebrate your little win. Make yourself proud.Be bold and loud. Wake up early. Sip your beautiful beverage and feel every single sip. First, second and so on. Grow every single day. Just smile while see yourself in mirror. Be your own inspiration. And let other inspire with your million dollar smile. Nourish yourself. Make some time for your own. Make art. Or whatever which peace and joy. Because your happiness means alot. And you deserve better. Don't expect from someone to be fit in your life according to you. Let them do whatever they love. Be a good person. Life is short but you are one who can make it sweeter day by day. Have fun and joy.

©Priya Manchanda.

# RADHIKA CHEJARLA

## 1. "Life is beautiful"

My world of joy!
Heart is like a little bird which sings gladness.
A long caged bird sets free from darkness.
Soft like feather which is lighter.
Door are open to cheer up the best.
Celebrating each moment with the joy.
Help others to smile when there say no.
Happiness moments can never be forgotten.
Win and loosing weight is not in mind to fly.
Trust the self love and support yourself.
Tomorrow might be a bright day,
Don't punish for unnecessary spaces.
A fresh mind and hope turns a day good.
Gathering friends to meet companion.
Enjoy to the fullest by rejoicing life.

## RAMYA DEVI

### 1. "Happiness"

The key to happiness is being happy by
yourself,
I'll try to contribute joy to the world,
We are the source of our joy,
If we hope for happiness in the world,
Freedom is the world of joy

# R. HARINI

## 1. "Joyful days"

Happiness is like our joy
May be through anything
Like happy moments and spend time with each others
Most of them are happy and enjoying there life
But they leaves the happiness where we get from small things
With World's of Joy
Happy mood becomes happy time and happy day
It is like our soul
It comes from our bottom of heart
Life is like treasury
When what happens ,
It is not in our hands
Happiness it is around us
But we should find it
It will not comes to us
We should find it
Happiness is a simple thing
Where we get more things ,that we should learn
Stress ,tensions , sorrows ,worries ,these are like our daily routine
But happiness is also included in our day to day life
So happiness makes a person fit and happy
Joy ful life makes life better
Don't think about past and be happy
Happiness is an only way where we get fulfil energy and stamina

Be happy
It is our only one life which god gave to us
That we should make it useful and utilize the time begin
Life can begins with sorrow
But we should change to happiness

© R. Harini.

## 2. "Precious life time"

Joyful of happiness will become joyful time ,
Joyful times becomes joyful hours ,joyful hours becomes joyful day, joyful days becomes joyful week, joyful week becomes joyful months , joyful months becomes joyful year
Here is the happiness that
Happiness is filled with
World's of joy

© R. Harini.

## ROHITH ARYA

### 1. "World Of Joy"

World of joy, In this world full of Heartbreaks and Stress, She was my World Of Joy.
The home of mine where I wanted to stay forever. She was my Stress-buster and Backbone to all my Dreams and Ideas. She was the one who brought Life to me. The one who inspired me to be a better human. She was the who made me more Loving more Caring, more Understanding and more Alive.
She was my 'SIRI' and 'ALEXA'. She was a part of me. She the answer to all my questions and insecurities.
And someday we all will have someone like her/him because we are blessed to be human. We are blessed to LOVE and feel. Because we all deserve a "WORLD OF JOY" .

## 2. "I am not 'ME' nowadays"

And maybe it's all because of you.
This distance and communication gap between us makes me disturbed and incomplete.
Maybe I am running from acceptance of reality that I am vulnerable without you.
Maybe It's only me who is being affected.
And this is how it looks like.
When we were giving words, moon & stars to each others maybe it was only me who meant them.
May be I was never World of joy.
Maybe I can't count on you more on my hard time cause you ain't there anymore.
Maybe it's not that essential for you to get some time for me, to remember what you said back then.

Maybe it's high time that I gotta let you go so I won't be VULNERABLE anymore.
Maybe I gotta learn to deal shits alone now. No.
Actually I could handle things alone and I can. But I had you that time. But unfortunately the terms are different now. You are different now.
But I am still the same. I remember my words and I'll stand them.

Maybe we ain't gonna be We anymore. It's YOU and ME.
Maybe I'll be better off alone.
Maybe I gotta say this to you but we had Beautiful time together.

We won't be same again.

We'll meet.
We'll talk.
We'll have fun.
We'll hug each other.
We'll laugh together.
We'll love each other.

But we won't be same again.

© Rohith Arya.

## 3. "You have got me"

I know that you are strong enough,
And self sufficient but this is just to make you remind that you have got me too,

When things fall apart and you can't take it anymore,
You have got me to find a way out.

When nights start to scare you and loneliness eats you up,
You have got me to talk to through out.

When the so called society Pressurize you with the so called assumptions y'll have made,

When you got someone troubling you in your World of joy and taking your Peace out,
You have got me for showing him/her the right place in life.

You have got me to release that pressure with.

When you are getting troubled by anyone out there,
You have got me to kick one their fucking face.

When the thoughts and stress don't let you sleep,
You have got me to take a song pill for that.

You have got me in all your odds.

You have got me whenever you need me till the time I have got you in my life.
© Rohith Arya.

## R. ROSHINI ANITA

### 1. *MY SHANGRI-LA*

Being to Grandma's place is always a pleasure!
The memories of gold I gain here is my forever treasure!
O' That big Oak tree standing so tall and mighty,
Waves its big branches and welcomes us with gaiety.
What a scenario it is! The sweet smelling garden,
The butterflies & bees that come to visit them... An absolute Eden!
With the snow glazed mountains in the backdrop,
Our hearts smile, smelling the aroma from the nearby bakeshop.
Grandma's puppies give us unfathomable love!
Their woof-woof & wagging tails are a promise of fondness from above!
The puppies and I enjoy playing with the visiting hares,
Rarely do we have a guest who comes and scares,
A huge wolly ball, the Big Brown Bear!
The gurgling waters by the stream that splish-splash,
Glisten in the daylight with a sparkling flash!
The tulips, roses & lilacs fill the air with their fragrant scent,
Making the place idyllic and dreamy with a Disney bent!
Above all these, festivity is the reigning note, unifying us.
With overwhelming delight, peace & laughter, no sign of muss!
What more can I ask for, other than such bliss? And ahoy!
This place on earth is my Shangri-la, an absolute "World of joy" !
© R. Roshini Anita.

## R.SUBASHINI

### 1. "The world of joy"

MOM is the world of
joy
The relation nobody can
annoy
When I'm stressed and
felt lonely
She is the one talks to
me friendly
She is the first person
who boost up me
She is the angel to
be
The person who always
hold me In her heart
I know I'm wrong sometimes,I'm
trying to be smart
She take care of me and
gave me hug
who always wishes
me a luck
Finally she says it's
alright
those words make my
life bright
She is the world of joy to me!
© R.Subashini.

## 2. "I dream the world of happiness"

My heart doesn't believes that I'm in happiness
Everytime my mind pops-up some sadness,
I don't know what it was
I don't know what it cause,
My mind tells everything should be change
But I don't know what to rearrange,
So I start dream the world of joy
That nobody can destroy,
That world should be filled with true souls
Which has no hole.

## 3. "Joy"

When we are tensed & felt lonely
Our childhood memories
Bring smile in our mouth
It brings kinda peace in our heart.

Joy is the only thing that make
our mind,peace in our irritation,
Only joy can bring the releif
in our stress.

The world of joy throw out your
dark and it exposes your glory,
When our battery (soul) is about to die
In a lack of energy (stress,pain),
Joy boost you up in a power saving mode.

© R.Subashini.

## SAKSHI CHAMAT

### 1. "Family is many things"

A family is many things.
With endless words that show
who they are and what they do
and how they teach you so you know.

But don't be weary if it's broken
or if through time it's been so worn.
Families are like that –
they're split up and always torn.
Love does not grow on every tree,
Nor true hearts yearly bloom.
Alas for those who only see
This cut across a tomb!
But, soon or late, the fact grows plain
To all through sorrow's test
talk
we laugh
we cry
but we are a family
and we do it all together
for as a family
we do it all as one
Picture's change to colour
Black and white has gone
A different place, a different time

World Of Joy

So much to look upon
Love your family while they are here
Keep their love very near
Family can leave the world at any time
So don't make yourself feel like slime
Family's forever and this I know
Friends enter your life and then they go
Making friends is fun trust me with this
But not something you would miss
So quickly life can take a turn,
Yet slowly we do seem to learn.
For same as night does turn to morn,
An untouched blanket can get torn,
We would all sit at the table
Everyone in their place
There were never any surprises
We recognized every face
Sometimes we feel rejected
by people who do not care,
but our hearts are warmed when remembering
that our family is always there!
Family is
one in itself; my love is your love.
Your pain is my pain, my wealth is your wealth.
I promise to never leave you by yourself.
Family is world of joy
forgiveness and patience.
It's sweeter than the sweetest fragrance.
The power of family is a reflection of God's compassion and magnificence.

## 2. "It was perfect situation"

It was a perfect situation,
Beyond my imagination.
Never knew how time passed by,
As i was just looking at her eye.
Both of us shared our secrets,
Without any regrets.
Cold breath of her, made me shiver,
Like in the wind of winter.
You are the keeper of my dreams,
The man who holds my heart,
The one I want to spend my life with,
The one with whom I will always stand.
Stand beside through thick and thin
Through all that life throws our way
Knowing that this special love we share
Will guide us each and every day.
I don't think you could ever feel
All the love I have to give,
It seems world of joy
And I'm sure you never realize
You've been my will to live.

## 3. "You are the one"

You gave light to my soul
You gave beats to my heart
You helped me to be whole
You taught me to be yours
I have felt love for you
And it will be more and more

You are the light when there is no sun.
You are the rainbow after the rain is done.
You are the star that twinkles in the night.
You are the moon that glows so bright.
You are the wind that whistles my name.
You are the love when the world is the same.

© Sakshi Chamat.

## SAPNA .P

### 1. "Money VS Morals"

One rupee was very famous in 1970's.Hundred rupees was most prestigious in 1980's.Thousand rupees was in full swing of zamindar's and rich people of 1990's .In 21st century ,India has become one of the developing countries because 70% people possesses moral values and 30% of people flattered by money .But after some time, people thought that, "Money is their life, Money makes them powerful and proud in front of society". Money changes their mind and makes them lacks in understanding the moral values. In life of Poor people, they wish that ," A survey of 2020 says that ," the black money has it's high influence on Indians ". Do we really get pride for having a lot of money in this "world of joy" ?
I would say that , A life with lacks with moral values ,there life would not in the form of bed of roses,The one who experienced the moral values would do the daily analyses for what they have spent, limited amount of savings ,A day with full potential of work, small surprises, minute crashes is enough for them. Not only the money makes them happy, if a person spends their nights with no pressure, no thinking about his safeguard of money in locker,finally no more money minded person; the one who possesses the moral values is equal to happiness of one who having the billions of money.

## 2. "THE WORLD OF JOY"

It's difficult to express about love
Experience and exploration
Is the special part in love
Understanding and expanding
Is the key for a healthy love
I have seen many lovers in beach
I have seen many lovely couples in court
One place is to express their love
Other place is to estimate their love
90's love is like a love between
Sea and tides, They won't get separated
The love of 2k kids is like a love between
Two friends, They won't give up for each other
In toss of a coin,Either head or tail
In toss of life,Either positive or negative
In toss of love,Neither for me nor for you.

© Sapna .p

## 3. "That one thing I still remember"

Me and my father, went to an ice-cream shop and he bought me my favorite ice-cream. I felt so happy, because after many months, I went for a ride with my dad.
Suddenly, a girl aged 6 or 7, came to me and asked to give my ice-cream.I was shocked and I don't know how to react, My heart decided to give but my mind refused because if dad comes and ask me," Without saying to me, how will you share?".
I couldn't take decision.Soon my father came, that girl went away from me.I don't know how to say this to my dad,but I decided to tell him.And I was so surprised for that answer, "Sapna, in this world, people are measured on two things, one is based on money ,other thing is humanity. If you loose your humanity, you don't deserve to live.We can see many beggers,but we are not that much rich to help all.But if we come across someone like that, surely we need to help them.On that moment, you will be treated as a God for them.So, God is there in You. No matter whether, I beat you or not?,but you should not give up your humanity in this "world of joy ".
From then, I decided to serve for society, I wish to God that, " I don't want to be a egoistic, aggressive or a selfish person. I want to be a person with helping tendencies and humanity".

# Saurabh Sant Gyaneshwar Khobragade

## 1. "Love"

Love is a part of life the love began person the world of joy in life...

## 2. "Success"

Every success made you joy and happy to enter successful life the world of joy in life..

## 3. *"Joy

The world of joy see mother and father face smile through any successful person...

## SHASWAT SOURAV SAHOO

### 1. "The Two Strangers"

She was sorry, disheartened
She apologized
It wasn't her mistake
Neither was it mine

She encapsulated all my sight
Never in my dream
I had such a beautiful exquisite
I handled myself with all my might.

It had happened
We bumped upon each other
I was with my files
She with pulchritudinous smiles

She left after a while
I couldn't let down my sight
But went through the nile
Chasing the alluring smiles

With each baby step to the right
The sound echoed,damped
My heart skipped being fright
Bring that angel along my sight

Broken me, stranger she
Everything collapsed
Uttered my conscience
We laid as two strangers
No contacts transcribed
With no paperback recite

Bit of paper she had left
Charmed my eyes again with light
Enthusiasm, ardour besieged me
No longer are we

© Shaswat Sourav Sahoo.

## 2. "The Two Strangers"

And everything gonna be alright.
"They met each other after 10 years following this incident and the bond between the strangers turned into bridal knot and Eventide.In this World of joy with ups and downs together they fight".

© Shaswat Sourav Sahoo.

## 3. "The Divine Soul"

In this world of joy that shine,
She was divine
Created beautifully by the destine
The only and exclusive one
Made for being only mine

She had the charm of sun
Sweetness of honey
Fragrance of lavender
And hangover of wine

Her hairs fluffed and rushed
Her body was of desirous kind
So engaging was her flawless skin
That even made snatched a glance of blind

I was caged inside her
She created a home inside me
She was my everything
She was the creation, the seraphic
Flaunting Transcendent and angelic smile

She hovered in my daydreams
Her presence made nightmares memes
She was different and distinct
Jim-dandy and peachy keen concocted her shrine

Realised me, One fine morning
Lost in her superficial beauty
Was an illusion of mine

## World Of Joy

The key to success and being uncaged
Was to assassinate the the lock
That never meant to be confined.

The Ace opened the door, the multihued azure
Was waiting for me to turn the alpha baseline.

## 4. "Time to Shine"

I loved her from all my heart
Leaving no place
For others to be a part
Yet she broke my heart

Besieged by grief and sorrows
Rejected me, pain followed
Depressed was me and broken
My definition for love verbally narrowed
I stood up and had my head
Staright and nothing to fear ahead
It's just a lesson that made me fed
Gear up boy, the champ within you
Has been unleashed
Lengthen your stride
And bounce yourself to the peak
Clutching all your pride
In this world of joy to ride.

# SHUMAILA AKHTAR

## 1. "The world of joy"

My world of joy is in your eyes
Because your eyes tell me the reason of my life,
Moon and sun
Whenever you are with me its lot of fun,
My smile shines brighter than the sunlight
Because you are the reason for every laugh in my life..!

## 2. "Your voice"

The world of joy is in your mind,your heart, your choice
Make it your strength,
Or others will be your voice..!

© Shumaila akhtar.

## 3. "Composite"

In this world of joy darkness and light both are opposite
If you can find the difference,
Then make yourself composite..!

© Shumaila akhtar.

# SHYAMA SHIVANI MISHRA

## 1. "NATURE- THE HEALER"

Thee enter into the world of joy ,
What if you are not getting that love.

If love from a mortal become insufficient,
Thee choose the place of ancient.

Have a look on the nature you are ignoring,
You will get much of love, unbearably.

Look at that sky,who is asking you for a smile;
Have a glance on the sun for a while.

The trees are ready to give a shade,
These kind of love, thee remain unpaid.

Have you ever thought of to be a poet?
And want to take a seat and stay quiet.

Love is not about to be with someone every time,
You can find the romance anywhere, anytime.

Nature will stay loyal and faithful,
You should rather choose a garden or river over people.

## 2. "SOULMATE"

When you are all in chaos and
And suddenly someone comes,
hugs you and says with a finality, "Don't worry. I'm here.
Everything will be fine, I will be your world of joy "
His voice firm and composed.
You want to ask, "What do you know about my fears and insecurities?"
But you can't ask or say anything and start sobbing in his arms.
What an ecstatic feeling! His arms so soothing!
Then you stop sobbing and look into his eyes,
Those deep, dark, beautiful eyes.
The eyes you never forget.
You stare at each other for sometime.
You both get lost into each other.
He grabs your waist and pulls you closer,
You are submissive and close your eyes.
Your lips are inches away from his.

The next moment your lips are on his. Such a tender touch!

And then you wake up.

© Shyama Shivani Mishra.

## SIMRAN KAUR

# 1. "The World of Books"

There are various things which make various sorts of blessings for various varieties of people. Everyone has their own taste, inspiration and inclination which contributes to their world of joy.

"You know you've read a good book when you turn the last page and feel a little as if you have lost a good friend."- Paul Sweeney.

I know it's a cliché but no one can deny that books are the best friends. Often they can lead you to some people who become your best friends too eventually.

Every reader has a journey. And in that he has a beginning, where he held a book in his hands for the very first time and was enchanted.

"The story is truly finished - and meaning is made - not when the author adds the last period, but when the reader enters." - Celeste Ng.

The mentioned quote becomes even more special when it's regarding that first ever book which we read. Often we readers have a reason while picking up a specific book which we wish to devour, but most of the cases our first book was just a beautiful accident. I remember I was a kid of around three or four, when a very good friend of my dad visited us. And he brought along with him something which changed my life for ever. He had bought me a set of "Children's classics collection" - a whole box filled with two dozens of little classic books. And it was 'Cinderella' which I picked up first! And after I finished all the books in that box, there was no turning back, and reading became my life. I had entered a paradise.

"I have always imagined that paradise will be a kind of library." - Jorge Luis Borges

A reader's world of joy is a place of peace, contentment and an always unsatiated craving for books. We are never tired of reading, reading again, yet again, and then pausing, wondering, relating, smiling and then getting back to reading, and reading further...! It's always what lies ahead that pull us and what lies behind wrenches us. And sometimes we live long with a book , beyond that book. Some statements are so special that we want to use drums and sing them aloud. It seems so important to tell everyone about that what one statement meant !

"Sometimes, you read a book and it fills you with this weird evangelical zeal, and you become convinced that the shattered world will never be put back together unless and until all living humans read the book." - John Green, The fault in our stars .

We readers are often accused of not interacting with the real world and are even assumed to be someone who doesn't likes to talk . I'm sure many of my fellow readers would have felt sorry for those who think that way . For those who might have never realised what an actual true conversation is and have never partaken in one !

"Reading is like a  conversation. All book speaks. But a good book listens as well."- Mark Haddon

Books are not mere pleasures. They are peacefully powerful weapons which are capable of igniting a new Renaissance at any time ! Each good book , written by a good writer , and read by a good reader and then shared with peers is a reform in its own self.

"Let us remember : One book, one pen, one child, and one teacher can change the world."- Malala Yousafzai

Books are definitely for learning and enhancing. However, they are at times simply for reflecting. It's not always someone else's story that we are reading. At times it's our very own one. At times books can be a mirror - bitter or sweet, that may depend.

"Maybe this is why we read, and why in moments of darkness we return to books: to find words for what we already know." - Alberto Manguel

I can go on and on when it comes to books, but let's end it here so that you may get a chance to read something worthy. And trust me, a book won't disappoint you ever!

Books are the best, beyond all limits. "The world of joy" for me is "the world of books".
After all, "The world was hers for reading." - Betty Smith
© Simran Kaur.

# S. KUMAR. S

## 1. "World of Joy"

It was first day of my college,
She was on her seat,  Me on mine. Though not nearby but we were close enough to see each other in zoom mode. It was the touch, feel, slice into my heart that first day itself. Yes people call it love at first sight. Joyous world.

I was trying to garner her vision at me but all in vain. This way week one, month one, quarter one passed, but no progress. Maybe it my fault. My shy nature couldnt arrest her though I dreamt of her every single day. My world of joy.

One fine day, she glanced at me. I attempted as if I knew nothing. She peeped towards me during the class. Was it a validation or LovE only God knows, my mind inquired with my heart. My joyful world.

I send her a message, wanting to meet in person. She replied saying 'Why, Where and What for?? I affirmed her, after the last class i will be waiting at the nearby resto 'The Water'. Wanting joy in my world.

It was 4pm and I was in reserved table seat, glancing the menu card. After an hour of patience, (as if I knew ~ God will send her to me today for sure), a sweet voice echoed by my earlobes 'can I sit here'. It was her. The super gorgeous, lady of my eyes. Joy struck in my world.

World Of Joy

We ordered two cups of cappuccino, with dark choco cookies. Our mild whispered chit- chats begun. I confessed directly, I like..

Her swaying long silky hairs,
Her silent deep lovely eyes,
Her smiling beautiful face,
Her simple talk - walk style,
Her look back into me moods.
Her joy made my world.

She got touched inside, deep in her soul with my true to heart words. Without anymore wait, she moved towards me. She touched my hands and her jasmine perfume blew me away. She was coming closer to me sec after sec, whereas myself as usual a shy- shy guy still. Me joyful or joyless lass.

All of a sudden, she touched her barefoot to mine and with those up-down slides, she transmitted electric currents into my nerves. She slide back and kissed on my cheecks. The joy of my world trippled.

The resto background music was playing d magic in my heart. All credit to the timeless beauty nearby me. She blew the musical chores in my ears while she inquired for my response to her urge in romantic eyes. She wanted me to take the guard now. Joyous moments calling?

And with heavy body, I tried my natural first go. I got into my zone, did hug her from one of the side. She gasped my hands towards her upper belly plus - the lower chest. She was in a cotton white top and blue skirt that day. She further pushed me up. As my fingers rolled on, upwards towards her , mountainous tracks. she felt the magic in her heart as I took circles on the hilly patches. Wanting me to press the wheat soft dough, I gently massaged her as fire was lit at both the ends. There was no look back. It felt as if we were on a long drive since ages knowing everything about each other as the comfort zone evolved among us. Joy was riding in every cell of my body.

Next, she moved my gentle fingers downwards under her belly. She loved my courtyard passing of her dense and dark grassland to fulfill her urge, as i felt like bungie jump into the valley. I couldn't stop as the wind blew both of us into the waterfall, my fingers deeply soaked into her hot spring wells. The volcano of white lava splashed out in a strike of second. She breath big and hold herself tight onto me. Our eyes came direct in contact with each other. What a connect was it. Heavens fell on earth that moment. Joy joy and joy all over.

In the meantime, my flight was ready for takeoff too. She was smart enough to guess and without any wait, she decided to fly the jet. I opened the main doors and after the welcome greet by two airhostess at the entrance door, she proceeded for her seat in the cockpit. Joyride gets ready.

The propeller had begun and engine was on fire too. With no mercy she put the right gears, moving up & down, to fly high the boeing into the heaven. At last the natural water showers cooled down my engine as we travelled smoothly to our destination. Joy fly in space.

Who knew the first love meet would be the experience of

fantasy ride of my life. The deep love we had though never revealed, did connect our souls and transmit right vibes bringing joy, ecstacy and love in us. The feelings in our hearts and souls blossomed that day. That was real joy real love of our lives. No boundaries, no limitations, no excuses. It was pure love, amazingly magical, insane and blind. Our filled with joy all around and in us

© S kumar S .

## SAMIYA KAGDI

### 1. The World of Joy

The world of joy is where I'm sitting;
musing upon,
left, right, forward, back, through,
the wind is blowing profusely,
slapping me upon face,
as making me aware of myself,
don't be so much traumatic,
this is mere a flood,
due to imbalance in nature emerges out,
you be balanced with,
be in acute harmonity,
stay where you nebulize with the multitution,
but you a humanbeing : a universal,
mandated to live compulsively,
encircling yourself,
In those inflictions,
you're the only who has to find the way,
out of such heart rendering incompatible frictions,
otherwise progressing ahead its charm,
engulf you intrusively,
won't give a single chance to construe,
but to complex the matter further,
It is you,
who has to see everything through your eyes,
rather than anyone's lended ones,

with those eyes,
you only would see : them,
Not you.
You : an essential and of a value creature;
keep in functioning mode all your senses,
merge all in unison,
and proceed straight,
where you can see through your self-made angle,
not through measurable degrees,
but something that comprises both : concreteness and essence.
Where you between two pathways;
one : where everything is green and yellow,
light emitting at,
A spark embodied into star,
indicating your eyes the way,
you frame your dream here.
Since then;
you saw yourself to be the part of this,
stepping into your own journey,
as with alteration an albino whale is coming out of the water, thriving himself upwards at full length,
as throwing a wishing star in the sky,
contributing a gift of sprouting,
solid bubbles again diving deep down into the water without bursting out,
tempered all droplets,
emerging out with the mountainous flesh
@Samiya Kagdi

# SP SMRUTI RANJAN PATI

## 1. "Love taught me"

Love taught me
How beautiful the journey in world of joy
Despite of this broken life
You left me with broken heart
With a just simple misunderstanding
Am here to answer all your queries,
Am still waiting .

Am still waiting ,
For your text
every time I see a notification
I wish it would be yours
But my wish stays with a wish
Because you are far away from me
And am at the past.

## 2. "World of joy"

We've all heard, love is this and love is that.
To you, I'm just a stranger connected without even knowing each other.

© Sp smruti ranjan pati.

## 3. "Memories"

Memories always remain
in the world of joy
And the last thing
Hey dear
Don't you feel the same
I always ask a question to myself..!!

## SNEHALAKSHMI. P

### 1. "The World Of Joy is the World Of Joy"

Admiring the nature is a world of joy
Blessings of Almighty is a world of joy
Celebrating festivals is a world of joy
Decorating our favourite places is a world of joy
Establishing a thing is a world of joy
Felicitating others is a world of joy
Gaining Knowledge is a world of joy
Harvesting crops is a world of joy
Illustrating experiments is a world of joy
Joking is a world of joy
Knocking the desks on the last day of school is a world of joy
Lightening the lamp is a world of joy
Marching towards the betterment is a world of joy
Nourishing environment is a world of joy
Opposing the wrong path is a world of joy
Prospering in life is a world of joy
Qualifying for finals is a world of joy
Raising after fall is a world of joy
Singing is a world of joy
Thanking for what we have is a world of joy
Uplifting others is a world of joy
Vanquishing is a world of joy
Writing is a world of joy
Yielding seeds is a world of joy
Zooming all our boons in the World of Joy is the World Of Joy!

# SONAL PRAJAPATI

## 1. "My lifepartner"

In a world of full confusion
You are the one which is my compulsion
I carry all my desire
Because I want to be your fire
Having your hug in a day
It is like a shower in month of may
You carry my stuff all the time
Your every words matches words of mine
Your heart pumps thinking about me
Only this thing I can see, see, see
You are a true blessing to my life
I really really want to be your wife.
In this my new, world of joy
Only you are the one who thinks I am not a, toy.

## 2. "My world"

My day starts from you and end on you.
Everyone loves me for my nature
But who I loved is all matter.
Clearing all pain that i have
Dancing with me in the rain
Holding my hands on way
I just closed my eyes & run away
Drinking tea in same cup
Taking our career in up
Fighting for me in the ring
He always pay for what I bring
A behind hug from him
Remind me of everything
U always make me pride
U are the one who never lied,
Taking me with you on ride,
He always stays on my side.....
If I have my feelings of joy.
It's because of you Mr. Roy

© Sonal Prajapati.

## 3. "Lockdown Life"

My life during lockdown was still a lesson for people like me. The most precious thing that i always need was with me. Thats TIME. It now depend with whom I want to spend and how. I started making a list of my all my friends & colleagues (school, college, coaching, office). And I call one person each day most of them have nothing to do but they all shows that they are busy so didnt go forward to it. I stated spending my time to my writings and some knowledge gaining session. Now the people who don't have time for me then are calling me now that how Talented I am. I am really thankful to them. If they would have talk to me that time then I had totally wasted my time and not concentrated on my hobby of writing shaayari, poems, stories, quotes. All thanks to them. I created my world of joy in own way .

© Sonal Prajapati.

# SONY JAISWAL

## 1. "Nature"

My day starts with shining sun,
Chirping of birds when tune,
Breezy wind make me feel,
Calm and optimistic all day long,
Maybe that's nature love ,
Made me feel so,
I love to feel the same,
Every day , every morning in world of joy,
When Sun sets in west,
And the shimmers of moon,
Stars make me smile,
This is the world of joy to me

© Sony jaiswal

## 2. "Love"

My love for mom,
My love for my family
My love for my friends,
My love for my partner,
My love for little ones,
My love for animals,
My love for nature,
My love for gifts I got,
My love for gifts of nature,
Which I get every time,
My day is full of love and emotions,
Which make me confident,
Gives me strength in this "world of joy" to reach,
My goal every time..

© Sony jaiswal

## 3. "My heart"

It's tough to be strong ,
Everytime,
But If I am weak ,
I can't live,
So many things are there,
Which break me every time,
But single smile of baby,
Blossomed flowers,
Hardworking bee,
The world of joy,
Unstoppable force of wind,
Dropping rain water,
Shining sun and stars,
Gives me ray of light,
To work hard,
Even though I am not strong,
But I have the courage,
To live all alone ......

© Sony jaiswal.

## S. PRINITA MATHI VATHANA

# 1. "Find the joy of ordinary"

They say a person needs just three things to be truly happy in this world: someone to love, something to do, and something to hope for." "Without pain, how could we know joy?'.Yeah, it's true In my life it was hard to survive in this society. In my childhood, my parents are very supportive of me but my happiness is no longer to me when I was eight years old my mom expired. After that me and father only. he was very supportive of me. After some years I reached higher studies. So I left him alone but on the other side I want to study for my dad because he is the only one for me but fate always separates me from him My college life is gorgeous to me. In my class I and two girls are hostels. Then we two became friends also. We three are always together only. we enjoyed our glorious days. I weekly went to see my father. I saw my father and after that, I return to my college but unfortunately, I met with an accident. I don't know what's happening to me but someone carrying me to the hospital after four hours later, I gained consciousness and one person standing before me and I woke up and asked, "who are you? ", It was one boy, he smiled at me and asked, "are you okay, are hurt anywhere ", and then I said I'm okay after that I got discharged from hospital. He dropped me. After that accident we became friends and we were very close. And I finish my final year and got selected in placement also. I got a job. This was happy news to me, I wanted to share it with my dad. So I called my dad and he was very happy. I said" I like one person dad ".In beginning he did not accept him after my marriage he accepted him. After few years he and my father passed away. Today I have nobody but I have backbone yes it's the twin babies. When I get tired they both smile at me I feel like an angel. God even took my mother, father and husband also but given my stamina yes it's my babies. Today I Survived in this society it's only my parents and my husband and god. My babies are " the world of joy".

© S.Prinita Mathi Vathana.

## 2. "You are worthy of love"

When the mind is pure, joy follows like a shadow that never leaves; yes it's true because my world of joy is my mother and dad. They made my life colourful like a rainbow. But girls of certain ages only live with their parents. After that, they lead to another life. When I get married, I want to leave my parents. That day was happy for all of you but it was a dark day for me. But my husband treated me like a child only. He is very supportive of me. But my In-laws were jealous and angry because of my husband's behaviour. He doesn't care about anything. He is a very quiet person. One day" I asked him why he loves me a lot?".He just smiled and replied to me. Because, your my crush and I blushed he noticed that, I asked him who is your first love? He replied me in school days to college days I was a playboy, I flirted with many girls and I got irritated he laughed at me are you jealous? I said no but He smiled at me all girls are not like you because my heart is yours. When I got pregnant, I was very happy. I wanted to share this happy news with my husband but he went on a business trip. When He returns I want to tell him. But my parents and mother-in-law scold me what are you doing you have to say this good news to your husband but I refused. I went to the airport to pick up my husband and that day He came with one girl and that girl was his first love. I was broken-hearted and I returned to my home, I was crying in my room. He came to my home to convince me but I was not ready for that and asked you if you wanted a divorce. He cried to me no I don't want a divorce. Why are you not ready to understand me. I said I want to divorce him. He also accepted divorce. We are divorced also. Few months after I went for a checkup the doctors said your water pot is getting dry. I got nervous but the doctors said don't worry take more water and take some medicine it's not serious it's a common problem for pregnant ladies. So I went to the shop to buy fruits for myself. On that day I saw my ex-husband's first girlfriend, she came with somebody she saw me, I refused her. But she followed me and she said I want to tell you the truth. On that day at the airport, you mistook your husband. I asked what are you saying? She said me I was GM for his company, so I and your husband went for a business trip but that day I don't know you came to pick up your husband so you misunderstood him. A few days ago I saw him he was miserable. So I asked him what happened to you?"He said everything to me, So I want to tell you the truth, After that, he said you two got divorced and you are pregnant. So I wanted to find you to tell the truth but my plans went wrong. Now I got relieved from this sinful feeling. I asked her, where is he said, she said I take her to him but, "unfortunately I got labour pain, so she took me to the hospital one person came to me and hold me. Take over to the operation theatre. In the operation theatre, one person was holding my hands he said push !push!baby is coming I was unconscious. After the surgery, I woke up but my baby is not beside me. So I asked my family members asked where is my baby they said wait, one person carrying my baby, yeah it's my handsome husband, I cried out sorry I mistook you. He replied don't say sorry because it was a terrible scene, leave it but from today onwards I won't leave you until my death. After that, my husband and my baby came together. That time I felt like I'm in "the world of joy "

© S.Prinita Mathi Vathana.

## 3. "Joyful life"

A person has needed two things love and joy. when you had these two things in your life, you feel a river moving in you, this is "the world of joy".

© S.Prinita Mathi Vathana.

## SRIJA SADHUKHAN

### 1. "VIE"

Light up the passage that left
Life is all about keep going
Enjoy the miracle of this beautiful world
Filling colour in the world of joy.
Life is a colorful bouquet of happiness
Bounded with ribbon of hope
Stop chasing others to seek happiness.
There is no place for sadness
Find happiness within yourself and
Happiness need to be created.
As everything is temporary on earth
Whether it may be sadness or happiness
Try to burn all negativities.

## STEFY HENSI.

### 1. "THE WORLD OF JOY"

Love is “ World of Joy ”!
Having the devil of lie ,
Compress the pumping blood,
To a drying up flood .

Which doesn't depends on what swallow,
When our mind is pure;
Joy follows us like shadow,
Which never leaves, ensure

© Stefy Hensi.G

## 2. " THE WORLD OF JOY"

The world of joy is full of pasture,
Tears of joy that moisture;
The road of sorrow that finished in narrow,
In the great world of joy, there is sneer;
That we cannot cure the world of sorrows,
Yet we can to choose to live in cheer!
Led in with joy and gladness;
Beautiful in it's loftiness,
The joy of whole earth;
The sadness chased away his mirth,
Genuine mirth in unblinking gaze;
Let joy fly everywhere for a days!..

© Stefy Hency.G

## STEPHY JULIYA. G

### 1. "Expectations in world of joy"

Once upon a time there lived a family in a small village. It was a small family consists of father, mother and a daughter. The name of the daughter was Anne. Anne was a twelve years old girl. She was very much loved by her parents since she is the only daughter to her parents. Anne's father provided all that she wants though they were a middle class family. Her father never regretted her desires. He always tried to fulfill her wishes. Anne loved her parents so much that she never hides anything from her parents.Her parents were the world of joy to her. Anne always wanted to see her parents with a smiling face. She always had a dream that, she has to work hard and make her family a luxurious one.

One day when Anne was doing her homework suddenly she remembered that her father's birthday was nearing. Anne wanted to give her father a great surprise. She planned to hang balloons and various colour papers to decorate her home. Anne wanted to make her father's birthday a remarkable one. She told her mother all about her plans for her father's birthday. Her mother also agreed to it. Anne and her mother worked together to make the day special.

The birthday of her father was nearing very soon. Anne was very excited and was also busy in making preparations for her father's birthday. On the day of Anne's father birthday Anne and her mother did not wish her father because they have a very big surprise for him in the evening. On that day morning, Anne's father went to work as usual. As soon as Anne's father went to work, Anne and her mother started decorating home. Anne prepared a delicious cake by herself for her father. Anne thought that her father would like this surprise that he will never forget it in his lifetime. Anne expected that surely her father would like this surprise.

It was almost 5pm. It was the time for Anne's father to return home. Anne and her mother were eagerly waiting for her father's arrival. It took very long time for father to come home. The time was 8pm but Anne's father did not return back home. But still Anne wass waiting for her father's arrival. It was almost 10 pm when Anne's father returned back home. Anne's father came home with full tension. When Anne's father entered into the home Anne pop the balloon were colorful tiny papers shattered over her father. This made him anger and he shouted at Anne. He started scolding her with harsh words. Which made her feel very bad. Anne expected that her father would like the surprise and the cake which she made fir him. But all that happened was opposite to all that she expected. All her expectations went in vain. Anne was very sad, she did not expect this from her father on his special day. She expected a happy face of her father. But all she saw was a anger face. All her expectations was a disappointment to her.

© Stephy Juliya. G

# SUBHASHINI VENKATESAN

## 1. "My World of Joy!"

Let we question ourselves first what's the meaning of Joy? Yeah, according to number of people's we have numerous meaning for the word Joy. And here is my world of Joy!

My Joyness arises with non-others its totally with myself and my parent's. First we should know what's the real meaning of Joy? Am Ria from Gurgaon and am belonged to a middle class family but my dreams are more than my status it didn't took me years to realise my real life style. I have understood my status in this pandemic situation. My parents were suffering a lot without getting work and salary they can't even afford money for my studies. Actually I thought myself as a fairy queen girl but some how this breakdown thought me am not a fairy queen girl am just a little poor girl but my heart can't take it so easy it just made my heart so painful. I questioned my Mother, What's the meaning of Joy? She just smiled with a tears and stepped to me and gave a tight hug and said the meaning of Joy is you my dear Riya!

It's almost a big turning point of my life and I asked my mom, Do you trust me? She said yes dear with my whole heart. I just holded my mother's hand and asked her to trust me that we will surely come out of this financial issues Soon and asked her to permit me to take Spoken English classes for school students cause am very good in spoken English at first Mumma was not okay with me then she said yes okay dear! Yeah, I have started to grow with my talents and dreams and now I can tell that's am a fairy queen girl with a stupendous Joy! My family is my world of Joy, I don't want it to break.

# SUKANYA M NAIR

## 1. "As Far as I Concern"

The emotion evoked by well-being!
The prospect of possessing!
The expression; a state of happiness;
A cause of delight,
Beatitude, blessedness, bliss, fuzziest,
Felicity, gladness, happiness,
Warm may sound the same as noun -
But difference forms the emotions.
It's getting hard in the worst of all!
The worst – quoted by the one,
Whom we yell the most!
Nevermore the word manifested -
But noted by me, yet didn't react.
Something that secures praise or renown,
That is what the "World of Joy"

## SUMANDRITA PAUL

### 1. "We purple you bts"

The seven stars of the seoul
To whom we are the only
Armies and though.....
There loves and emotions
Inspires us.....
Where'as they are ready to give
There heart's as well as there life too only for us........

There presentation and outfits
Heals our heart,
There dances and songs
Which make us feel;
There love for us is unconditional.
We purple you seven jewel's....
As armies are always
in our heart....
No matter what happens...
Armies are there for all,
As you all are the shining
Stars or in other words
the seven heros of the "world of joy".

## 2. "Blackpink in your area"

The queens are pretty savage
As we know them
They are the one and only
Blackpink of the game.

No matter what happens
They are the revolution
Blackpink is always there
To keep u happy
Forever.......

Whether its jennie or jisoo
Whether its lisa or rose
They all have a strong bonding,
In each and every moments though...
Even the "world of joy" couldn't break their intimacy and bonding..!!

## 3. "World of joy"

When i was small enough;
In every single beat I thought
That if i have a fantasy
To become an imaginary.
I would go to a dreamland
To fulfill my all dreams in
In my life.....
No matter what happens
If i have abstacles in my life.

In a beautiful moon night,
Sitting alone beside a pond where
The splash of light from the moon
Falls over the pond.

Thinking in a dream that
I ll go and stay in a land
Where the place would be
Filled with beauty peace
With a shine.

There i ll make a house
Of bricks and few straws
For as i ll stay and
Watch the whole view of
The nature that goes on.......

And rather i ll have a
Pond of lotus;
Where i ll sail in a boat

Forever......
And little ducks roaming
About....
And a bridge which is filled
With flowers and all.......

And when the evening comes
In all
The blue sky then turns
Into a purple glow and all.....
And with shining stars
Above the sky,
Looking like a heaven of
The fly's......

Then on and all with
Grassy fields.....
A blowing air comes
Towards on it....
Then slightly swings
And node's their
Heads....
Where a fantasy gurll
watches all
This view alone in her
Way.

© Sumandrita Paul.

## SUMATHI PALANISAMY

### 1. " One day in World of joy"

One day you will not receive my text Or calls One day my feelings for you will fade One day your fragrance will not freeze me One day you will know how I loved you One day you I will not be more by your side One day my broken heart will fixed One day my tears for you will vanish One day my available will be unavailable One day my efforts for you will stop One day I will forget everything And be in joy with my successful carrier

## 2. "Why ?"

Why you thought me what is correct and wrong
Why you thought me to go on the correct path
Why you thought how to face the society
Why you thought me not everyone are the same
Why you thought me how to handle the situation
But why don't teach me that you're the one
Why don't teach me to survive without you
Why don't teach me that you're passing cloud
Why don't you teach me to move on without you
Why don't you teach me to be strong without you
Why left me ?

© Sumathi Palanisamy.

## 3. "World of joy"

In the world of joy I am being alone In the world of bright I am being in the dark In the world of selfish I am being a sacrifice everything In the world of moving time I am being in the same movement In the world of fake I am being true In the world of hating I am being hurt In the world of enjoyment I am being searched for joy
And perhaps world full of joy.

© Sumathi Palanisamy.

# SYED NAZEERUNISA

## 1. "World of Joy"

If this great world of joy and pain
Revolve in one sure track;
If freedom, set, will rise again,
And virtue, flown, come back;
Woe to the purblind crew who fill
The heart with each day's care;
Nor gain, from past or future, skill
To bear, and to forbear!

## 2. "Infant Joy"

'I have no name;
I am but two days old.'
What shall I call thee?
'I happy am,
Joy is my name.'
Sweet joy befall thee!

Pretty joy!
Sweet joy, but two days old.
Sweet Joy I call thee:
Thou dost smile,
I sing the while;
Sweet joy befall thee!

## 3. "Joy and Pleasure"

Now, joy is born of parents poor,
And pleasure of our richer kind;
Though pleasure's free, she cannot sing
As sweet a song as joy confined.

Pleasure's a Moth, that sleeps by day
And dances by false glare at night;
But Joy's a Butterfly, that loves
To spread its wings in Nature's light.
Joy's like a Bee that gently sucks
Away on blossoms its sweet hour;
But pleasure's like a greedy Wasp,
That plums and cherries would devour.

Joy's like a Lark that lives alone,
Whose ties are very strong, though few;
But Pleasure like a Cuckoo roams,
Makes much acquaintance, no friends true.
Joy from her heart doth sing at home,
With little care if others hear;
But pleasure then is cold and dumb,
And sings and laughs with strangers near.

© Syed Nazeerunisa.

## TANYA GOYEL

### 1. "Artistic Scenario"

Let's have a vist in the World Of Joy

Everything being so perfect on the utopia globe.

Flawlessly people giving their own exertion and toil,
No jealousy with each other on this soil.

No Green Wars, and wars of gas and fire,
People roaming all around with brothers, forbiding conspire.

The world which gives view of paradise,
No mind gamed and everyone is live and no inlfation in price.

Absence of poverty and discriminatory challenges,
No case of suicide and truant terror and unkindness.

The planet looks like a star,
Beautiful and twinkling as always by no indeed demolishing nature.

That world of joy will be full of optimist people,
Where there is nay phobia from rapists.

The mart of power, the fount of will,
The source and bound of good and ill will be every evil.

## World Of Joy

The society having delirium,
When all the girls and boys  walks on road with equilibrium.
Free-minded from tensions and stress,
Everyone, from continuous work, will take some rest.

The world in which there is no case of  molestation and fight on vague,
Full of happiness where everyone's dignity has value.

Sharing love and concern with each and every country,
Living there, all'll be free,
If we truely wish to be.

© Tanya goyel.

## UMAMA SHAKEEL

### 1. "If I'm a boy in world of joy "

I would be a good naughty and mischevious boy who would be nice as well as considerate to all and especially to girls and women for I'm attracted towards them for everything they do be it my mother my sister or my girlfriend.
Actually i will be ever grateful to God and to woman for their life centres around me only and in return we can atleast respect them and be good to woman folk without whom I can't think of a day even
Most importantly I will be try to be sympathetic in their period days the pain the trauma they go through only for us if we think deep
Their all pain are for we boys only so when I'm a boy I will do my best to lessen it be it menstrual or her pregnancy problems as a boy I will
be more careful than ever for all the women in my life
But then I will not forget that I'm a boy quite privileged and so shall enjoy my life too which a girl seldom can do
I will grab this opportunity of being a boy a man and live life most gracefully respectfully and merrymaking too but without hurting anyone's sentiments beyond love

## VALLIKALA.C

### 1. "TIME"

In the introduction of Time
Some of the faces that stand forever in heart
Some of the faces that will disappear over time !!

There are some people who should not be forgotten !!
There are some people who should be forgotten !!

Time that connect some relationships !!
Sometimes showing no interest !!
Some misunderstanding relationship also there eventhough being together !!

Sometimes our desired paths and actual paths might not be different!!
Sometimes might end up with unexpected destinations !!

Let your joy be in your time of journey
Not in some distant goal ..!!
It will lead you to THE WORLD OF JOY !!!!

## 2. "LIFE"

Like Baby's scribblings, Various things in life
Which cannot be understood for sometime ,eventhough we drawn!!

The difference is here !!
We know the beginning and the end,
But not the ruling personality over those!!

Eventhough uncoloured ,
Baby's scribblings won't meet an end ...
Untill and unless it's blossoming hands get tired !!

But here,
To make a colourful rainbow,
Need to sow seeds with hardening hands eventhough dirt !!

Full of ups and downs here
like Irregular scribblings of child
That says, "Life won't be straight !!"

Eventhough meaningless,
Giving some moment of
immense pleasure !!!

We cannot cure the world of sorrows,
But we can choose to live in "THE WORLD OF JOY"

© Vallikala.C

## 3. "IF YOU WERE, I WOULD BE"

If you were colour,
I would be a rainbow,
So You can be different versions of yourself within me !!!

If you were the rainbow,
I would be sky,
So I can carry you in my lap all the time !!!

If you were the sky,
I would be twinkling stars ,
To enhance your beauty !!!

If you were the stars,
I would be Eyes
to look forward to seeing you for my entire life

If you were the Eyes,
i would be Light,
to make you admire the things in the world !!

If you were the Light,
I would be the path
So We both will lead to
The world of joy..!!

© Vallikala.C

# VAISHNAVI KUMARI

## 1. "Never ever give up in the world of joy "

Despite all the hurdles, obstacles, failures nd negativities u must never succumb to them in fact keep moving on. You will always find a way if you pro

# VAISHNAVI RAJESH NAIK

## 1. "The World of Joy for a newborn"

The world of joy for a baby is seeing his loved ones beside. The world of joy for the babies is getting care and love from his/her family. The world of joy for the baby is living in the space of no restrictions.

The world of joy for a baby is learning and experimenting new things. The world of joy for a baby is deriving nourishment and courage from people beside him/her.

## 2. "The world of Joy for an adult"

The world of joy for an adult is creating and having his/her own space. The world of joy for an adult is building as many strong and unique bonds with his/her school and college mates. The world of joy for an adult is the place reached after overcoming the tough phases. The world of joy for an adult is the right to speak and express his/her towards anyone/ anything. The world of joy for an adult is witnessing his decisions moulding the health of his/her surroundings. The world of joy for an adult is persuing what he/she adores.

## 3. "The world of joy for elderly"

The world of joy for the elderly is seeking prosperity for his/her family. The world of joy for an elderly is continuing to do what he did throughout his life. The world of joy for an elderly is following the path towards serenity and togetherness. The world of joy for an elderly is seeing his/her grandchildren conquering their master world. The world of joy for elderly will be staying mentally healthy forever.

© Vaishnavi Rajesh Naik

# VARSHINI

## 1. "My world"

My world is filled with joy, you can say it's a world of joy. Yes, when I started by own business after giving up my competitive exams I felt joy, happiness even if I earn a little bit money it's always gave me happiness. Even I get one customer a day I was not stressed while I was doing my competitive exams I always felt stress  pressure I was not even willing to write competitive exams eventhough I put all my hardwork studied day and night. But ended up getting stressed, cried endless nights, dreams become dark but when I started doing my own business ya it's true it's a small business it gave me joy. I entered into the world of joy. That's when I felt whatever you do. You must need to love it then even the work is hard it will not be hard for you. It's always a joyful one for us when we do the work we do.

© Varshini.

## 2. "Joy of writing"

When I started writing I didn't even expect I will turn into a writer, I started writing small quotes in social media by friends and the followers encouraged me that gave me motivation to write . Writing is the world of joy why because I cam express all the feeling even I can't able to say out but I can make it into poems. I can express my heart out no one is going to stop. The freedom in writing gaves me joy and happiness. When I own compitations it encourages to write more. I don't want depend on anyone nowadays but whatever I feel I make it into writings. Well the secret are kept as secrets and a good writing is also came up two in one.writing is a world of joy. If you wanna feel then start writing

© Varshini.

## 3. "Friendship"

Friendship,
The ship of joy,
The World of happiness,
The world of joy,
The ship of endless love,
No destination for this ship,
This ship never sinked,
This ship carries tones of joy,
This ship carries tones of memories,
The ship that we choose to travel,
The ship we can travel without any problems,
Friends is a sea in the world of joy

© Varshini.

# VARUN KESARIA

## 1. "Human's sire bond : HUNGER IN WORLD OF JOY"

Hunger does it all,
Hunger plays the game;
Hunger for food makes us crave,
Hunger for money makes us slave.

We creatures are bound to hunger,
It teaches bird to fly;
It teaches Child to cry;
It teaches human to lie.

We creatures are sired to hunger,
To satisfy hunger, we give our best;
Choosing the good path creates the heavenly bliss,
Choosing the bad path creates the deadly wish.

Hunger has it all,
Hunger plays the game;
It's best side makes poor, the rich;
It's worst side makes rich, the poor.

Never get the greed of hunger,
It may make you regret.
Satisfy the hunger with what you have,
It may change your fate.

## 2. "Dark night"

Every new day, brings a part of it;
For some it may be sorrow,
For some it may be sweet.

It brings with itself,
Lots of thoughts & lots of dreams;
Where there will be laughs;
Where there will be screams.

Some will be horrific,
Some might be terrific;
Some may give us pain,
Some might put a strain.

Some full of love,
Some full of happiness;
Some full smiles,
Some full of tears.

A part of day, with starry sky;
Where we rule the world, where we may cry;
Where some will stay awake, where some will sleep tight;
You guessed it right ! It's a dark night in world of joy .

© Varun Kesari.

## 3. "Me Being Mysogynist"

I met a girl,
Looked like queen;
She was a mingler,
Her look was keen.

I fell in love with her,
She accepted my rose;
Life was about to cheer in world of joy ,
But then I became the cause.

She attracted me,
By her looks;
She talked so sweetly,
That caged me in her hooks.

She brought the twist,
And I was lost.
She turned out to be a sinner
And so mean.
She cheated on me,
And showed me the grave;
This is the truth,
Which brought me the death.

This was the tale,
Of a girl;
Who came into my life,
And made it hell.

© Varun Kesari.

# V. LOURDU CATHERINE

## 1. "My golden movements in world of joy"

A golden day makes more golden happy movements to be remembered throughout the entire life. Once they lived a girl named Jenifer she loves to do many social activities and also she helps each other. One day she was in her second year of her college, she joined the NSS group where she can perform many social activities. Jenifer took part in various events conducted by the NSS group. The college to motivate students decided to arrange a camp of seven days Jenifer actively participated in the camp. As soon as they reached the camping spot the trainer decided the troop into five groups to do their activities. Jenifer was in the first group and his troop enjoyed the camp and travel by playing and singing songs. After starting their first day of the camp Jenifer and her friends got the first work of their camp to distribute the pamphlets to make awareness to the people around the village. The first day of the camp ended happily with lots of fun and memories. The next two days students were requested to make the cleaning works all over the campus. They also planted new many trees; they also interacted with each other and got many friends from the different departments. They all enjoyed the camp with lots of happiness. They fellow the next two days the students were worked to clean the whole village which made Jenifer and her friends happier. The village people were also so happy and welcomed the students with lots of lots. Jenifer was also happy to do service for the village people. As days passed nearly seven days they completed their camp of the world of joy and also shared their joy with each other. Thus, Happiness can be felt everywhere and the only thing are to find it in each and everything that is happening around the world.

"Spread love, Spread happiness,
Spread the essence of joy
Throughout world".

© V. Lourdu Catherine.

## YASMIN AAMIR AMEEN

### 1. "World of Joy!"

I imagine it as a world where people live happily,
A world where there is no politics,
A world where people have no jealousy among them,
A world where everyone is respected,
Everyone is judged equally,
A world without rapes,
A world where everyone is in peace,
A world without fights and wars,
A world of Joy is my imaginary world
Where everything nice happens!

## 2. "World of happiness!"

Happiness isn't available anywhere
You have to find it in you
It can be found in situations and people too
Be happy and make others happy too
Because the happiness in making others happy is an awesome feeling
You cannot buy it
For some it comes easy
Others have to chase for it
Happiness is a gem
The one who has it is lucky
It is a feeling, an emotion, a blessing...
Happiness is bliss indeed!

© Yasmin Aamir Ameen

## 3. "A world of fun n frolic!"

A world of fun and frolic,
Where children play all day,
Their naughtiness makes everyone smile,
Their blabbering all day is like music to the ears,
Children make the world look so beautiful,
They are a blessing,
A gift from God!
Children are a world of Joy!

© Yasmin Aamir Ameen

# YOGESH GURJAR CHINU

## 1. "This series"

The wind will pass through me,
Now my feelings will wreak havoc,

My compulsions are immense
This cycle does not stop,

I am angry with myself, sit silently,
Even then the chain of tears does not stop,

Memories have become my stories,
Now my moment does not cut,

The scene doesn't say anything
The questions are no longer answered,

The restlessness of my heart increased,
There is no solution now

Tired now the pupils of the eyes,
The wait that doesn't stop....!!

© Yogesh Gurjar Chinu.

## 2. "Enjoy the Rain"

Saw unseasonal rain in the scorching sun,
When I saw the clouds coming,

Only one thought came to my mind,
The attention came to take the gram flour,

Know what is the real identity of rain,
A person welcomes with tea and pakodas,

Invited friends home over tea,
Made them taste with tea and dumplings,

Everyone likes corn in the rain,
The fun is when everyone has eaten and gathered,

Then made a program with friends,
While bathing in the rain, he ate corn on a handcart,
We made this rain a memorable one,
We made some moments of life joyful....!!

© Yogesh Gurjar Chinu.

## 3. "My Unfinished Tales"

My circumstances were very complicated.
Some unfinished tales of mine buried,

I wanted some things,
Now there is a stir in my emotions,

The sea which had stopped for my tears,
Now it will flow freely, will shed my emotions,

Tell me many unfinished tales,
Time runs away, my moment does not stop,

The process of gatherings had stopped,
Now the direction of the winds will change,

He said that I have to be separated now,
I also did not stop him, did not stop him since when,

Let the liver do you with anonymous love,
Would have stopped but the river of pain does not stop with anyone...!!

© Yogesh Gurjar Chinu.

# YUVASREE. P

## 1. "World of Joy"

World of Joy,
No one can lead a life without tasting the bitterness of sorrow.
Yes, life is a combination of happinness, sadness, surprise and adventure.
One has to come across pain and struggles to win the bread named "Success"

## 2. "Success in world of joy "

"Success is not final unless you have learnt from your failures"
Life is short and temporary, so live the life as you wish and enjoy it to the fullest!

## 3. "Joyful World"

'The world joy is joyful. There is something called Good and Bad! But the option is Yours! Choose it wisely'.

© Yuvasree.

# ZEENAT

## 1. " A letter to you "

When we meet in this world of joy, I just found something special between you and me
Something above this world's imagination that you never can see

You never come much closer too me
But I can feel your heartbeat
I can feel the vibe of your face
The drug in your eyes
In memories, that always leave a beautiful trace

I always found the relaxation in your wonderful smile
You never have the sense to get ready
But I always love your style

The way you breath
The way you see
That give me a freshness
Like a good morning tea

Something is present between you and me
I have seen it, but you never see...!!

## 2. "Teddy bear"

Teddy bear teddy bear
Turn around
Come and hug me
And heal my wound

Teddy bear teddy bear
Listen to me
My words are my feelings
That you can understand only

Teddy bear teddy bear
Please wipe my tears
Give me some sympathy
And make me forget my all fears

Teddy bear teddy bear
Love me please
You are the only one
Who only sees
Teddy bear teddy bear
Give me a smile
Come to me, remove my sadness
And make me agile

Teddy bear teddy bear
Just look at me
Give me your soft lap
Because I want to sleep

Teddy bear teddy bear

World Of Joy

You are the best
In this world of joy, You always present me in every condition
And heal my pain without any rest.

© Zeenat.

## 3. "Don't tie in relationships"

Say hey to the life
Say bye to the dark
Go into light
And in night, you can see the stars

In this world of joy, You are there alone
But still happy and smiling
No one is present to stop you
Do whatever you are willing..

But still you can't be there forever
You have something else
Your some relationships are alive
That can be called heaven or hell

You have to stop
Cut your feathers
Some relations you have
For them you have to step back rather.
Relationships are the feelings
That can't count in words
But don't make them your barrier
Become a flower from their buds

Don't tie in relationships
You have your own life
Uphold them
But don't make them your dream killer knife...!!

© Zeenat.